ADMISSION TEST SERIES

THIS IS YOUR **PASSBOOK**® FOR ...

PROJECT MANAGEMENT PROFESSIONAL (PMP)

NATIONAL LEARNING CORPORATION®
passbooks.com

COPYRIGHT NOTICE

This book is SOLELY intended for, is sold ONLY to, and its use is RESTRICTED to individual, bona fide applicants or candidates who qualify by virtue of having seriously filed applications for appropriate license, certificate, professional and/or promotional advancement, higher school matriculation, scholarship, or other legitimate requirements of educational and/or governmental authorities.

This book is NOT intended for use, class instruction, tutoring, training, duplication, copying, reprinting, excerption, or adaptation, etc., by:

1) Other publishers
2) Proprietors and/or Instructors of «Coaching» and/or Preparatory Courses
3) Personnel and/or Training Divisions of commercial, industrial, and governmental organizations
4) Schools, colleges, or universities and/or their departments and staffs, including teachers and other personnel
5) Testing Agencies or Bureaus
6) Study groups which seek by the purchase of a single volume to copy and/or duplicate and/or adapt this material for use by the group as a whole without having purchased individual volumes for each of the members of the group
7) Et al.

Such persons would be in violation of appropriate Federal and State statutes.

PROVISION OF LICENSING AGREEMENTS. — Recognized educational, commercial, industrial, and governmental institutions and organizations, and others legitimately engaged in educational pursuits, including training, testing, and measurement activities, may address request for a licensing agreement to the copyright owners, who will determine whether, and under what conditions, including fees and charges, the materials in this book may be used them. In other words, a licensing facility exists for the legitimate use of the material in this book on other than an individual basis. However, it is asseverated and affirmed here that the material in this book CANNOT be used without the receipt of the express permission of such a licensing agreement from the Publishers. Inquiries re licensing should be addressed to the company, attention rights and permissions department.

All rights reserved, including the right of reproduction in whole or in part, in any form or by any means, electronic or mechanical, including photocopying, recording, or by any information storage and retrieval system, without permission in writing from the Publisher.

Copyright © 2018 by

NLC®

National Learning Corporation

212 Michael Drive, Syosset, NY 11791
(516) 921-8888 • www.passbooks.com
E-mail: info@passbooks.com

PUBLISHED IN THE UNITED STATES OF AMERICA

PASSBOOK® SERIES

THE *PASSBOOK® SERIES* has been created to prepare applicants and candidates for the ultimate academic battlefield – the examination room.

At some time in our lives, each and every one of us may be required to take an examination – for validation, matriculation, admission, qualification, registration, certification, or licensure.

Based on the assumption that every applicant or candidate has met the basic formal educational standards, has taken the required number of courses, and read the necessary texts, the *PASSBOOK® SERIES* furnishes the one special preparation which may assure passing with confidence, instead of failing with insecurity. Examination questions – together with answers – are furnished as the basic vehicle for study so that the mysteries of the examination and its compounding difficulties may be eliminated or diminished by a sure method.

This book is meant to help you pass your examination provided that you qualify and are serious in your objective.

The entire field is reviewed through the huge store of content information which is succinctly presented through a provocative and challenging approach – the question-and-answer method.

A climate of success is established by furnishing the correct answers at the end of each test.

You soon learn to recognize types of questions, forms of questions, and patterns of questioning. You may even begin to anticipate expected outcomes.

You perceive that many questions are repeated or adapted so that you can gain acute insights, which may enable you to score many sure points.

You learn how to confront new questions, or types of questions, and to attack them confidently and work out the correct answers.

You note objectives and emphases, and recognize pitfalls and dangers, so that you may make positive educational adjustments.

Moreover, you are kept fully informed in relation to new concepts, methods, practices, and directions in the field.

You discover that you arre actually taking the examination all the time: you are preparing for the examination by "taking" an examination, not by reading extraneous and/or supererogatory textbooks.

In short, this PASSBOOK®, used directedly, should be an important factor in helping you to pass your test.

EXAM CONTENT OUTLINE

The following table identifies the proportion of questions from each domain that will appear on the examination. These percentages are used to determine the number of questions related to each domain and task that should appear on the multiple-choice format examination.

Domain	Percentage of Items on Test
I. Initiating the Project	13 %
II. Planning the Project	24 %
III. Executing the Project	30 %
IV. Monitoring and Controlling the Project	25 %
V. Closing the Project	8 %
Total	100%

For educational purposes from the official announcement
© Project Management Institute, Inc. All rights reserved.

PERFORMANCE DOMAIN I: INITIATING THE PROJECT

Domain I	Initiating the Project – 13 %
Task 1	Perform project assessment based upon available information and meetings with the sponsor, customer, and other subject matter experts, in order to evaluate the feasibility of new products or services within the given assumptions and/or constraints.
Task 2	Define the high-level scope of the project based on the business and compliance requirements, in order to meet the customer's project expectations.
Task 3	Perform key stakeholder analysis using brainstorming, interviewing, and other data-gathering techniques, in order to ensure expectation alignment and gain support for the project.
Task 4	Identify and document high-level risks, assumptions, and constraints based on current environment, historical data, and/or expert judgment, in order to identify project limitations and propose an implementation approach.
Task 5	Develop the project charter by further gathering and analyzing stakeholder requirements, in order to document project scope, milestones, and deliverables.
Task 6	Obtain approval for the project charter from the sponsor and customer (if required), in order to formalize the authority assigned to the project manager and gain commitment and acceptance for the project.
	Knowledge and Skills:[A] • Cost-benefit analysis • Business case development • Project selection criteria (for example, cost, feasibility, impact) • Stakeholder identification techniques • Risk identification techniques • Elements of a project charter

---

[A] In addition to domain-specific knowledge and skills, these specifications include a set of cross-cutting knowledge and skills used in multiple domains. The cross-cutting knowledge and skills list is found in the section on Cross-Cutting Knowledge and Skills.

For educational purposes from the official announcement
© Project Management Institute, Inc. All rights reserved.

Performance Domain II: Planning the Project

Domain II	Planning the Project – 24%
Task 1	Assess detailed project requirements, constraints, and assumptions with stakeholders based on the project charter, lessons learned from previous projects, and the use of requirement-gathering techniques (e.g., planning sessions, brainstorming, focus groups), in order to establish the project deliverables.
Task 2	Create the work breakdown structure with the team by deconstructing the scope, in order to manage the scope of the project.
Task 3	Develop a budget plan based on the project scope using estimating techniques, in order to manage project cost.
Task 4	Develop a project schedule based on the project timeline, scope, and resource plan, in order to manage timely completion of the project.
Task 5	Develop a human resource management plan by defining the roles and responsibilities of the project team members in order to create an effective project organization structure and provide guidance regarding how resources will be utilized and managed.
Task 6	Develop a communication plan based on the project organization structure and external stakeholder requirements, in order to manage the flow of project information.
Task 7	Develop a procurement plan based on the project scope and schedule, in order to ensure that the required project resources will be available.
Task 8	Develop a quality management plan based on the project scope and requirements, in order to prevent the occurrence of defects and reduce the cost of quality.
Task 9	Develop a change management plan by defining how changes will be handled, in order to track and manage changes.
Task 10	Plan risk management by developing a risk management plan, and identifying, analyzing, and prioritizing project risks in the risk register and defining risk response strategies, in order to manage uncertainty throughout the project life cycle.†
Task 11	Present the project plan to the key stakeholders (if required), in order to obtain approval to execute the project.

For educational purposes from the official announcement
© Project Management Institute, Inc. All rights reserved.

Task 12	Conduct a kick-off meeting with all key stakeholders, in order to announce the start of the project, communicate the project milestones, and share other relevant information.
	Knowledge and Skills:[B] - Requirements gathering techniques - Work breakdown structure (WBS) tools and techniques - Time, budget, and cost estimation techniques - Scope management techniques - Resource planning process - Workflow diagramming techniques - Types and uses of organization charts - Elements, purpose, and techniques of project planning - Elements, purpose, and techniques of communications planning - Elements, purpose, and techniques of procurement planning - Elements, purpose, and techniques of quality management planning - Elements, purpose, and techniques of change management planning - Elements, purpose, and techniques of risk management planning

† This task was updated in August 2011 as a result of feedback from the project management community and validated by the PMP RDS Task Force and Certification Governance Council (CGC).

[B] In addition to domain-specific knowledge and skills, these specifications include a set of cross-cutting knowledge and skills used in multiple domains. The cross-cutting knowledge and skills list is found in the section on Cross-Cutting Knowledge and Skills.

For educational purposes from the official announcement
© Project Management Institute, Inc. All rights reserved.

PERFORMANCE DOMAIN III: EXECUTING THE PROJECT

Domain III	Executing the Project – 30 %
Task 1	Obtain and manage project resources including outsourced deliverables by following the procurement plan, in order to ensure successful project execution.
Task 2	Execute the tasks as defined in the project plan, in order to achieve the project deliverables within budget and schedule.
Task 3	Implement the quality management plan using the appropriate tools and techniques, in order to ensure that work is being performed according to required quality standards.
Task 4	Implement approved changes according to the change management plan, in order to meet project requirements.
Task 5	Implement approved actions and follow the risk management plan and risk register, in order to minimize the impact of negative risk events on the project.†
Task 6	Maximize team performance through leading, mentoring, training, and motivating team members.
	Knowledge and Skills:[c] - Project monitoring tools and techniques - Elements of a statement of work - Interaction of work breakdown structure elements within the project schedule - Project budgeting tools and techniques - Quality standard tools - Continuous improvement processes

† This task was updated in July 2011 as a result of feedback from the project management community and validated by the PMP RDS Task Force and Certification Governance Council (CGC).

[c] In addition to domain-specific knowledge and skills, these specifications include a set of cross-cutting knowledge and skills used in multiple domains. The cross-cutting knowledge and skills list is found in the section on Cross-Cutting Knowledge and Skills.

For educational purposes from the official announcement
© Project Management Institute, Inc. All rights reserved.

PERFORMANCE DOMAIN IV:
MONITORING AND CONTROLLING THE PROJECT

Domain IV	Monitoring and Controlling the Project – 25 %
Task 1	Measure project performance using appropriate tools and techniques, in order to identify and quantify any variances, perform approved corrective actions, and communicate with relevant stakeholders.
Task 2	Manage changes to the project scope, schedule, and costs by updating the project plan and communicating approved changes to the team, in order to ensure that revised project goals are met.
Task 3	Ensure that project deliverables conform to the quality standards established in the quality management plan by using appropriate tools and techniques (e.g. testing, inspection, control charts), in order to satisfy customer requirements.
Task 4	Update the risk register and risk response plan by identifying any new risks, assessing old risks, and determining and implementing appropriate response strategies, in order to manage the impact of risks on the project.
Task 5	Assess corrective actions on the issue register and determine next steps for unresolved issues by using appropriate tools and techniques in order to minimize the impact on project schedule, cost, and resources.
Task 6	Communicate project status to stakeholders for their feedback, in order to ensure the project aligns with business needs.
	Knowledge and Skills:[D] <ul><li>Performance measurement and tracking techniques (for example, EV, CPM, PERT)</li><li>Project control limits (for example, thresholds, tolerance)</li><li>Project performance metrics (for example, efforts, costs, milestones)</li><li>Cost analysis techniques</li><li>Variance and trend analysis techniques</li><li>Project plan management techniques</li><li>Change management techniques</li><li>Integrated change control processes</li></ul>

[D] In addition to domain-specific knowledge and skills, these specifications include a set of cross-cutting knowledge and skills used in multiple domains. The cross-cutting knowledge and skills list is found in the section on Cross-Cutting Knowledge and Skills.

For educational purposes from the official announcement
© Project Management Institute, Inc. All rights reserved.

- Risk identification and analysis techniques
- Risk response techniques (for example, transference, mitigation, insurance, acceptance)
- Problem solving techniques (including root cause analysis)
- Reporting procedures

PERFORMANCE DOMAIN V: CLOSING THE PROJECT

Domain V	Closing the Project – 8 %
Task 1	Obtain final acceptance of the project deliverables by working with the sponsor and/or customer, in order to confirm that project scope and deliverables were met.
Task 2	Transfer the ownership of deliverables to the assigned stakeholders in accordance with the project plan, in order to facilitate project closure.
Task 3	Obtain financial, legal, and administrative closure using generally accepted practices, in order to communicate formal project closure and ensure no further liability.
Task 4	Distribute the final project report including all project closure-related information, project variances, and any issues, in order to provide the final project status to all stakeholders.
Task 5	Collate lessons learned through comprehensive project review, in order to create and/or update the organization's knowledge base.
Task 6	Archive project documents and material in order to retain organizational knowledge, comply with statutory requirements, and ensure availability of data for potential use in future projects and internal/external audits.
Task 7	Measure customer satisfaction at the end of the project by capturing customer feedback, in order to assist in project evaluation and enhance customer relationships.[9]
	Knowledge and Skills:[E] • Contract closure requirements • Basic project accounting principles • Close-out procedures • Feedback techniques • Project review techniques • Archiving techniques and statutes • Compliance (statute/organization) • Transition planning techniques

---

[E] In addition to domain-specific knowledge and skills, these specifications include a set of cross-cutting knowledge and skills used in multiple domains. The cross-cutting knowledge and skills list is found in the section on Cross-Cutting Knowledge and Skills.

For educational purposes from the official announcement
© Project Management Institute, Inc. All rights reserved.

CROSS-CUTTING KNOWLEDGE AND SKILLS

All Domains	Cross-Cutting Knowledge and Skills
	<ul><li>Active listening</li><li>Brainstorming techniques</li><li>Conflict resolution techniques</li><li>Cultural sensitivity and diversity</li><li>Data gathering techniques</li><li>Decision making techniques</li><li>Facilitation</li><li>Information management tools, techniques, and methods</li><li>Leadership tools and techniques</li><li>Negotiating</li><li>Oral and written communication techniques, channels, and applications</li><li>*PMI's Code of Ethics and Professional Conduct*</li><li>Presentation tools and techniques</li><li>Prioritization/time management</li><li>Problem-solving tools and techniques</li><li>Project management software</li><li>Relationship management</li><li>Stakeholder impact analysis</li><li>Targeting communications to intended audiences (for example, team, stakeholders, customers)</li><li>Team motivation methods</li></ul>

HOW TO TAKE A TEST

You have studied long, hard and conscientiously.

With your official admission card in hand, and your heart pounding, you have been admitted to the examination room.

You note that there are several hundred other applicants in the examination room waiting to take the same test.

They all appear to be equally well prepared.

You know that nothing but your best effort will suffice. The "moment of truth" is at hand: you now have to demonstrate objectively, in writing, your knowledge of content and your understanding of subject matter.

You are fighting the most important battle of your life—to pass and/or score high on an examination which will determine your career and provide the economic basis for your livelihood.

What extra, special things should you know and should you do in taking the examination?

I. YOU MUST PASS AN EXAMINATION

A. WHAT EVERY CANDIDATE SHOULD KNOW
Examination applicants often ask us for help in preparing for the written test. What can I study in advance? What kinds of questions will be asked? How will the test be given? How will the papers be graded?

B. HOW ARE EXAMS DEVELOPED?
Examinations are carefully written by trained technicians who are specialists in the field known as "psychological measurement," in consultation with recognized authorities in the field of work that the test will cover. These experts recommend the subject matter areas or skills to be tested; only those knowledges or skills important to your success on the job are included. The most reliable books and source materials available are used as references. Together, the experts and technicians judge the difficulty level of the questions.

Test technicians know how to phrase questions so that the problem is clearly stated. Their ethics do not permit "trick" or "catch" questions. Questions may have been tried out on sample groups, or subjected to statistical analysis, to determine their usefulness.

Written tests are often used in combination with performance tests, ratings of training and experience, and oral interviews. All of these measures combine to form the best-known means of finding the right person for the right job.

II. HOW TO PASS THE WRITTEN TEST

A. BASIC STEPS

1) Study the announcement

How, then, can you know what subjects to study? Our best answer is: "Learn as much as possible about the class of positions for which you've applied." The exam will test the knowledge, skills and abilities needed to do the work.

Your most valuable source of information about the position you want is the official exam announcement. This announcement lists the training and experience qualifications. Check these standards and apply only if you come reasonably close to meeting them. Many jurisdictions preview the written test in the exam announcement by including a section called "Knowledge and Abilities Required," "Scope of the Examination," or some similar heading. Here you will find out specifically what fields will be tested.

2) Choose appropriate study materials

If the position for which you are applying is technical or advanced, you will read more advanced, specialized material. If you are already familiar with the basic principles of your field, elementary textbooks would waste your time. Concentrate on advanced textbooks and technical periodicals. Think through the concepts and review difficult problems in your field.

These are all general sources. You can get more ideas on your own initiative, following these leads. For example, training manuals and publications of the government agency which employs workers in your field can be useful, particularly for technical and professional positions. A letter or visit to the government department involved may result in more specific study suggestions, and certainly will provide you with a more definite idea of the exact nature of the position you are seeking.

3) Study this book!

III. KINDS OF TESTS

Tests are used for purposes other than measuring knowledge and ability to perform specified duties. For some positions, it is equally important to test ability to make adjustments to new situations or to profit from training. In others, basic mental abilities not dependent on information are essential. Questions which test these things may not appear as pertinent to the duties of the position as those which test for knowledge and information. Yet they are often highly important parts of a fair examination. For very general questions, it is almost impossible to help you direct your study efforts. What we can do is to point out some of the more common of these general abilities needed in public service positions and describe some typical questions.

1) General information

Broad, general information has been found useful for predicting job success in some kinds of work. This is tested in a variety of ways, from vocabulary lists to questions about current events. Basic background in some field of work, such as sociology or economics, may be sampled in a group of questions. Often these are principles which have become familiar to most persons through exposure rather than through formal training. It is difficult to advise you how to study for these questions; being alert to the world around you is our best suggestion.

2) Verbal ability

An example of an ability needed in many positions is verbal or language ability. Verbal ability is, in brief, the ability to use and understand words. Vocabulary and grammar tests are typical measures of this ability. Reading comprehension or paragraph interpretation questions are common in many kinds of civil service tests. You are given a paragraph of written material and asked to find its central meaning.

IV. KINDS OF QUESTIONS

1. Multiple-choice Questions

Most popular of the short-answer questions is the "multiple choice" or "best answer" question. It can be used, for example, to test for factual knowledge, ability to solve problems or judgment in meeting situations found at work.

A multiple-choice question is normally one of three types:
- It can begin with an incomplete statement followed by several possible endings. You are to find the one ending which *best* completes the statement, although some of the others may not be entirely wrong.
- It can also be a complete statement in the form of a question which is answered by choosing one of the statements listed.
- It can be in the form of a problem – again you select the best answer.

Here is an example of a multiple-choice question with a discussion which should give you some clues as to the method for choosing the right answer:

When an employee has a complaint about his assignment, the action which will *best* help him overcome his difficulty is to
    A. discuss his difficulty with his coworkers
    B. take the problem to the head of the organization
    C. take the problem to the person who gave him the assignment
    D. say nothing to anyone about his complaint

In answering this question, you should study each of the choices to find which is best. Consider choice "A" – Certainly an employee may discuss his complaint with fellow employees, but no change or improvement can result, and the complaint remains unresolved. Choice "B" is a poor choice since the head of the organization probably does not know what assignment you have been given, and taking your problem to him is known as "going over the head" of the supervisor. The supervisor, or person who made the assignment, is the person who can clarify it or correct any injustice. Choice "C" is, therefore, correct. To say nothing, as in choice "D," is unwise. Supervisors have and interest in knowing the problems employees are facing, and the employee is seeking a solution to his problem.

2. **True/False**

3. **Matching Questions**
    Matching an answer from a column of choices within another column.

V. RECORDING YOUR ANSWERS

Computer terminals are used more and more today for many different kinds of exams.

For an examination with very few applicants, you may be told to record your answers in the test booklet itself. Separate answer sheets are much more common. If this separate answer sheet is to be scored by machine – and this is often the case – it is highly important that you mark your answers correctly in order to get credit.

VI. BEFORE THE TEST

YOUR PHYSICAL CONDITION IS IMPORTANT
If you are not well, you can't do your best work on tests. If you are half asleep, you can't do your best either. Here are some tips:

1) Get about the same amount of sleep you usually get. Don't stay up all night before the test, either partying or worrying—DON'T DO IT!
2) If you wear glasses, be sure to wear them when you go to take the test. This goes for hearing aids, too.
3) If you have any physical problems that may keep you from doing your best, be sure to tell the person giving the test. If you are sick or in poor health, you relay cannot do your best on any test. You can always come back and take the test some other time.

Common sense will help you find procedures to follow to get ready for an examination. Too many of us, however, overlook these sensible measures. Indeed, nervousness and fatigue have been found to be the most serious reasons why applicants fail to do their best on civil service tests. Here is a list of reminders:

- Begin your preparation early – Don't wait until the last minute to go scurrying around for books and materials or to find out what the position is all about.
- Prepare continuously – An hour a night for a week is better than an all-night cram session. This has been definitely established. What is more, a night a week for a month will return better dividends than crowding your study into a shorter period of time.
- Locate the place of the exam – You have been sent a notice telling you when and where to report for the examination. If the location is in a different town or otherwise unfamiliar to you, it would be well to inquire the best route and learn something about the building.
- Relax the night before the test – Allow your mind to rest. Do not study at all that night. Plan some mild recreation or diversion; then go to bed early and get a good night's sleep.
- Get up early enough to make a leisurely trip to the place for the test – This way unforeseen events, traffic snarls, unfamiliar buildings, etc. will not upset you.

- Dress comfortably – A written test is not a fashion show. You will be known by number and not by name, so wear something comfortable.
- Leave excess paraphernalia at home – Shopping bags and odd bundles will get in your way. You need bring only the items mentioned in the official notice you received; usually everything you need is provided. Do not bring reference books to the exam. They will only confuse those last minutes and be taken away from you when in the test room.
- Arrive somewhat ahead of time – If because of transportation schedules you must get there very early, bring a newspaper or magazine to take your mind off yourself while waiting.
- Locate the examination room – When you have found the proper room, you will be directed to the seat or part of the room where you will sit. Sometimes you are given a sheet of instructions to read while you are waiting. Do not fil out any forms until you are told to do so; just read them and be prepared.
- Relax and prepare to listen to the instructions
- If you have any physical problem that may keep you from doing your best, be sure to tell the test administrator. If you are sick or in poor health, you really cannot do your best on the exam. You can come back and take the test some other time.

VII. AT THE TEST

The day of the test is here and you have the test booklet in your hand. The temptation to get going is very strong. Caution! There is more to success than knowing the right answers. You must know how to identify your papers and understand variations in the type of short-answer question used in this particular examination. Follow these suggestions for maximum results from your efforts:

1) Cooperate with the monitor
The test administrator has a duty to create a situation in which you can be as much at ease as possible. He will give instructions, tell you when to begin, check to see that you are marking your answer sheet correctly, and so on. He is not there to guard you, although he will see that your competitors do not take unfair advantage. He wants to help you do your best.

2) Listen to all instructions
Don't jump the gun! Wait until you understand all directions. In most civil service tests you get more time than you need to answer the questions. So don't be in a hurry. Read each word of instructions until you clearly understand the meaning. Study the examples, listen to all announcements and follow directions. Ask questions if you do not understand what to do.

3) Identify your papers
Civil service exams are usually identified by number only. You will be assigned a number; you must not put your name on your test papers. Be sure to copy your number correctly. Since more than one exam may be given, copy your exact examination title.

4) Plan your time
Unless you are told that a test is a "speed" or "rate of work" test, speed itself is usually not important. Time enough to answer all the questions will be provided, but this

does not mean that you have all day. An overall time limit has been set. Divide the total time (in minutes) by the number of questions to determine the approximate time you have for each question.

5) Do not linger over difficult questions

If you come across a difficult question, mark it with a paper clip (useful to have along) and come back to it when you have been through the booklet. One caution if you do this – be sure to skip a number on your answer sheet as well. Check often to be sure that you have not lost your place and that you are marking in the row numbered the same as the question you are answering.

6) Read the questions

Be sure you know what the question asks! Many capable people are unsuccessful because they failed to *read* the questions correctly.

7) Answer all questions

Unless you have been instructed that a penalty will be deducted for incorrect answers, it is better to guess than to omit a question.

8) Speed tests

It is often better NOT to guess on speed tests. It has been found that on timed tests people are tempted to spend the last few seconds before time is called in marking answers at random – without even reading them – in the hope of picking up a few extra points. To discourage this practice, the instructions may warn you that your score will be "corrected" for guessing. That is, a penalty will be applied. The incorrect answers will be deducted from the correct ones, or some other penalty formula will be used.

9) Review your answers

If you finish before time is called, go back to the questions you guessed or omitted to give them further thought. Review other answers if you have time.

10) Return your test materials

If you are ready to leave before others have finished or time is called, take ALL your materials to the monitor and leave quietly. Never take any test material with you. The monitor can discover whose papers are not complete, and taking a test booklet may be grounds for disqualification.

VIII. EXAMINATION TECHNIQUES

1) Read the general instructions carefully. These are usually printed on the first page of the exam booklet. As a rule, these instructions refer to the timing of the examination; the fact that you should not start work until the signal and must stop work at a signal, etc. If there are any *special* instructions, such as a choice of questions to be answered, make sure that you note this instruction carefully.

2) When you are ready to start work on the examination, that is as soon as the signal has been given, read the instructions to each question booklet, underline any key words or phrases, such as *least, best, outline, describe*

and the like. In this way you will tend to answer as requested rather than discover on reviewing your paper that you *listed without describing*, that you selected the *worst* choice rather than the *best* choice, etc.

3) If the examination is of the objective or multiple-choice type – that is, each question will also give a series of possible answers: A, B, C or D, and you are called upon to select the best answer and write the letter next to that answer on your answer paper – it is advisable to start answering each question in turn. There may be anywhere from 50 to 100 such questions in the three or four hours allotted and you can see how much time would be taken if you read through all the questions before beginning to answer any. Furthermore, if you come across a question or group of questions which you know would be difficult to answer, it would undoubtedly affect your handling of all the other questions.

4) If the examination is of the essay type and contains but a few questions, it is a moot point as to whether you should read all the questions before starting to answer any one. Of course, if you are given a choice – say five out of seven and the like – then it is essential to read all the questions so you can eliminate the two that are most difficult. If, however, you are asked to answer all the questions, there may be danger in trying to answer the easiest one first because you may find that you will spend too much time on it. The best technique is to answer the first question, then proceed to the second, etc.

5) Time your answers. Before the exam begins, write down the time it started, then add the time allowed for the examination and write down the time it must be completed, then divide the time available somewhat as follows:
   - If 3-1/2 hours are allowed, that would be 210 minutes. If you have 80 objective-type questions, that would be an average of 2-1/2 minutes per question. Allow yourself no more than 2 minutes per question, or a total of 160 minutes, which will permit about 50 minutes to review.
   - If for the time allotment of 210 minutes there are 7 essay questions to answer, that would average about 30 minutes a question. Give yourself only 25 minutes per question so that you have about 35 minutes to review.

6) The most important instruction is to *read each question* and make sure you know what is wanted. The second most important instruction is to *time yourself properly* so that you answer every question. The third most important instruction is to *answer every question*. Guess if you have to but include something for each question. Remember that you will receive no credit for a blank and will probably receive some credit if you write something in answer to an essay question. If you guess a letter – say "B" for a multiple-choice question – you may have guessed right. If you leave a blank as an answer to a multiple-choice question, the examiners may respect your feelings but it will not add a point to your score. Some exams may penalize you for wrong answers, so in such cases *only*, you may not want to guess unless you have some basis for your answer.

7) Suggestions
   a. Objective-type questions
      1. Examine the question booklet for proper sequence of pages and questions
      2. Read all instructions carefully
      3. Skip any question which seems too difficult; return to it after all other questions have been answered
      4. Apportion your time properly; do not spend too much time on any single question or group of questions
      5. Note and underline key words – *all, most, fewest, least, best, worst, same, opposite,* etc.
      6. Pay particular attention to negatives
      7. Note unusual option, e.g., unduly long, short, complex, different or similar in content to the body of the question
      8. Observe the use of "hedging" words – *probably, may, most likely,* etc.
      9. Make sure that your answer is put next to the same number as the question
      10. Do not second-guess unless you have good reason to believe the second answer is definitely more correct
      11. Cross out original answer if you decide another answer is more accurate; do not erase until you are ready to hand your paper in
      12. Answer all questions; guess unless instructed otherwise
      13. Leave time for review

   b. Essay questions
      1. Read each question carefully
      2. Determine exactly what is wanted. Underline key words or phrases.
      3. Decide on outline or paragraph answer
      4. Include many different points and elements unless asked to develop any one or two points or elements
      5. Show impartiality by giving pros and cons unless directed to select one side only
      6. Make and write down any assumptions you find necessary to answer the questions
      7. Watch your English, grammar, punctuation and choice of words
      8. Time your answers; don't crowd material

8) Answering the essay question

Most essay questions can be answered by framing the specific response around several key words or ideas. Here are a few such key words or ideas:

M's: manpower, materials, methods, money, management
P's: purpose, program, policy, plan, procedure, practice, problems, pitfalls, personnel, public relations
a. Six basic steps in handling problems:
   1. Preliminary plan and background development
   2. Collect information, data and facts
   3. Analyze and interpret information, data and facts
   4. Analyze and develop solutions as well as make recommendations

5. Prepare report and sell recommendations
6. Install recommendations and follow up effectiveness

b. Pitfalls to avoid
1. *Taking things for granted* – A statement of the situation does not necessarily imply that each of the elements is necessarily true; for example, a complaint may be invalid and biased so that all that can be taken for granted is that a complaint has been registered
2. *Considering only one side of a situation* – Wherever possible, indicate several alternatives and then point out the reasons you selected the best one
3. *Failing to indicate follow up* – Whenever your answer indicates action on your part, make certain that you will take proper follow-up action to see how successful your recommendations, procedures or actions turn out to be
4. *Taking too long in answering any single question* – Remember to time your answers properly

EXAMINATION SECTION

EXAMINATION SECTION
TEST 1

DIRECTIONS: Each question or incomplete statement is followed by several suggested answers or completions. Select the one that BEST answers the question or completes the statement. *PRINT THE LETTER OF THE CORRECT ANSWER IN THE SPACE AT THE RIGHT.*

1. _____ is commonly used to report on project performance.
   A. Earned Value Management
   B. WBS
   C. Quality Management Plan
   D. RBS

2. Which of the following is NOT a process associated with communications management?
   A. Distribute information
   B. Manage stakeholder expectations
   C. Plan communication
   D. Survey questionnaire

3. As a project manager, you are expected to make relevant information available to project stakeholders as planned. Which process does this relate to?
   A. Distribute information
   B. Manage stakeholder expectations
   C. Plan communication
   D. Report performance

4. Report performance involves all of the following EXCEPT
   A. collecting and distributing performance data
   B. collecting and distributing progress measurements
   C. collecting stakeholder information needs
   D. collecting and distributing forecasts

5. Of the following examples listed, which is a sign of feedback from the receiver?
   A. No written response from the receiver
   B. An acknowledgement or additional questions from the receiver
   C. Encoding the message by the receiver
   D. Decoding the message by the receiver

6. As a project manager you are expected to create a scope statement. Once you have the statement, you find it to be useful in all the following ways EXCEPT
   A. describing the purpose of the project
   B. describing the objectives of the project
   C. distributing information
   D. explaining the business problems the project is expected to solve

7. What are project deliverables?   7._____
   A. Tangible products that the project is expected to deliver
   B. Prioritized list of deliverables
   C. Project scope statement
   D. Project documents

8. As a project manager, you are arranging criteria for project completion criteria.   8._____
   You could organize it using all of the following EXCEPT
   A. functional department
   B. milestones
   C. tasks of projects
   D. project phase

9. Which of the following is not a task under "Developing human resource plan"?   9._____
   A. Documenting organizational relationships
   B. Looking for the availability of required human resources
   C. Identification and documentation of project roles and responsibilities
   D. Creating a staffing plan

10. If you are a project manager who is keen in managing a project team, you would   10._____
    undertake any of the following EXCEPT
    A. creating a staffing plan
    B. evaluating individual team member performance
    C. providing feedback
    D. resolving conflicts

11. Nurturing the team is a vital role of a project manager. If you have to do so, what   11._____
    would you avoid?
    A. Guide the team members as required
    B. Provide mentoring throughout the project
    C. Remove the team member who is found to be less skilled
    D. On-the-job training

12. War room creation is an example of   12._____
    A. co-location
    B. management skills
    C. rewards and recognitions
    D. establishing ground rules

13. The team member roles and responsibilities could be documented using all of the   13._____
    following EXCEPT
    A. functional chart
    B. text-oriented format
    C. hierarchical type organizational chart
    D. matrix-based responsibility chart

14. _____ is NOT an example of constraints placed upon the project by current organizational policies.
    A. Hiring freeze
    B. Reduced training funds
    C. Organizational chart templates
    D. Rewards and Increments Freeze

15. As a project manager, you have decided to have a virtual team. What kind of limitation would this create with regards to team development?
    A. Rewards and recognition
    B. Establishing ground rules
    C. Team building
    D. Co-location

16. Unplanned training means
    A. team building using virtual team arrangement
    B. competencies developed as a result of project performance appraisals
    C. on-the-job training
    D. training that is done without any planning in advance

17. Resource break down structure is an example of
    A. functional chart
    B. text-oriented format
    C. hierarchical type organizational chart
    D. matrix-based responsibility chart

18. A project manager would consider the following as inputs to define scope EXCEPT
    A. requirements document
    B. project Charter
    C. product management plan
    D. organizational process charts

19. Aldo is a project manager and has to terminate a project earlier than planned. The level and extent of completion should be documented. Under which is this done?
    A. Verify scope
    B. Create scope
    C. Control scope
    D. Define scope

20. Sam, an IT project manager, is having difficulty in getting resources for his project, and hence has to depend highly on department heads. Which type of organization is Sam most likely working with?
    A. Functional
    B. Tight matrix
    C. Weak matrix
    D. Projectized

Questions 21-25.

Len is a project manager of an infrastructure project manager of a well-known company. He is involved in various processes of scope management. Look at the following chart and align the different processes to various tasks listed. Choose the appropriate answer for each process and list them under corresponding tasks.

	Processes	Corresponding tasks	List of tasks
21.	Define scope	21._____	A. Monitoring project scope and project status
22.	Control scope	22._____	B. Defining and documenting stakeholder needs
23.	Collect requirements	23._____	C. Formalizing acceptance of the complete project deliverables
24.	Verify scope	24._____	D. Breaking down the project into smaller, more manageable tasks
25.	Create WBS	25._____	E. Developing a detailed description of the project and its ultimate product

---

KEY (CORRECT ANSWERS)

1. A
2. D
3. A
4. C
5. B

6. C
7. A
8. C
9. B
10. A

11. C
12. A
13. A
14. C
15. D

16. B
17. C
18. C
19. A
20. A

21. E
22. A
23. B
24. C
25. D

TEST 2

DIRECTIONS: Each question or incomplete statement is followed by several suggested answers or completions. Select the one that BEST answers the question or completes the statement. *PRINT THE LETTER OF THE CORRECT ANSWER IN THE SPACE AT THE RIGHT.*

1. In which of the following processes would risk be identified?
    A. Risk identification
    B. Risk monitoring and control
    C. Qualitative risk analysis
    D. Risk identification, monitoring and control

    1._____

2. Jack has prepared a risk management plan for his project and also identified risks in his project. Which of the following processes should Jack do next?
    A. Plan risk responses
    B. Perform qualitative analysis
    C. Perform quantitative analysis
    D. Monitor and control risk

    2._____

3. Which of the following is NOT a step in risk management?
    A. Perform qualitative analysis
    B. Monitor and control risk
    C. Risk identification
    D. Risk breakdown structure

    3._____

4. Sue is a project manager for an IT project at a corporate office. She is engaged in the process of identifying risks. To do so, she collects inputs from experts from the field through a questionnaire. What is this technique called?
    A. Interview
    B. Documentation review
    C. Delphi technique
    D. Register risk

    4._____

5. Positive risks may be responded by which of the following:
    I. Exploit   II. Accept   III. Mitigate   IV. Share

    A. I and III
    B. All of the above
    C. I, II and IV
    D. I, II and III

    5._____

6. Risk _____ is a response to negative risks.
    A. identification
    B. mitigation
    C. response plan
    D. management plan

    6._____

7. Which of the following statements is NOT true about risk management?
    A. Risk register documents all the risks in detail
    B. Risks always have negative impacts and not positive
    C. Risk mitigation is a response to negative risks
    D. Risk register documents the risks in detail

8. _____ is the document that lists all the risks in a hierarchical fashion.
    A. Risk breakdown structure
    B. Lists of risks
    C. Risk management plan
    D. Monte Carlo diagram

9. Nicole is a project manager of a reforestation project. In one of the project reviews, she realizes that a risk has occurred. Which document should Nicole refer to take an appropriate action?
    A. Risk response plan
    B. Risk register
    C. Risk management plan
    D. Risk breakdown structure

10. As a project manager, you have invited experts for an effective brainstorming session to identify risks involved in the project. What is the ideal group size?
    A. 3   B. 6   C. 4   D. 5

11. Of the following personnel, who is NOT involved in project risk identification activities?
    A. Clerical staff
    B. Subject matter experts
    C. Other project managers
    D. Risk management experts

12. _____ is one of the tools/techniques used in risk identification.
    A. Risk tracker
    B. Checklist analysis
    C. Risk register
    D. Project scope

13. Jim is a project manager in a bank. He is collecting input for the risk identification process. What input would he be collecting to identify risks?
    I. Project scope statement
    II. Enterprise environmental factors
    III. Project management plan
    IV. Diagramming techniques

    A. I and IV only
    B. III and IV only
    C. All of the above
    D. I, II and III only

14. Which of the following could a project manager collect from a risk tracker?
    I. Root causes of risk and updated risk categories
    II. List of identified risks
    III. Risk register
    IV. List of potential responses

    A. I and IV only
    B. III and IV only
    C. I, II and IV
    D. II only

15. The risk management plan should describe the entire risk management process, including auditing of the process, and should also define _____.
    A. reporting
    B. environmental factors
    C. organizational process assets
    D. project management plan

16. What do risk categories define?
    A. How to communicate risk activities and their results
    B. Types and sources of risks
    C. How risk management will be done on the process
    D. When and how the risk management activities appear in the project schedule

17. Which of the following is not a method of risk identification?
    A. Diagramming
    B. Interviewing
    C. SWOT
    D. RBS

18. Shauna is conducting a qualitative risk analysis for her project. What is she required to do?
    A. Apply a numerical rating to each risk
    B. Assess the probability and impact of each identified risk
    C. Assign each major risk to a risk owner
    D. Outline a course of action for each major risk identified

19. Which of the following is not a criterion to close a risk?
    A. Risk is no longer valid
    B. Risk event has occurred
    C. Risk activities are recorded regularly
    D. Risk closure at the direction of a project manager

20. As a project manager, you establish a risk contingency budget. Which of the following is not a purpose of establishing a risk contingency budget?
    A. To be reviewed as a standing agenda item for project team meetings
    B. To prepare in advance to manage the risks successfully
    C. To have some reserve funds
    D. To avoid going over the budget allotted

21. Which of the following statements is NOT correct in terms of designing a risk management?
    A. Risk is inherent to project work
    B. In any organization, projects will have common risks
    C. Some risks may occur more than once in the life a project
    D. Risks identified will definitely occur

22. All identified potential risk events that are viewed to be relevant to the project are to be recorded using the
    A. risk register
    B. risk management matrix
    C. risk report
    D. SOW

23. _____ is/are an example of a business risk.
    A. Poorly understood requirements
    B. A merger
    C. Introduction of new technology to the organization
    D. Work outside the project scope

24. Personnel turnover in a project is a
    A. Business risk
    B. Not a risk at all
    C. Technology risk
    D. Project risk

25. Which of the following is not an example of mitigation?
    A. Set expectations
    B. Involve customer in early planning process
    C. Provide training for personnel
    D. Hiring a backup person for a key team member

KEY (CORRECT ANSWERS)

1. D	11. A
2. B	12. B
3. D	13. D
4. C	14. C
5. C	15. A
6. B	16. B
7. B	17. D
8. A	18. B
9. A	19. C
10. A	20. A

21. D
22. B
23. B
24. D
25. D

TEST 3

DIRECTIONS: Each question or incomplete statement is followed by several suggested answers of completions. Select the one that best answers the question or complete the statement. *PRINT THE LETTER OF THE CORRECT ANSWER IN THE SPACE AT THE RIGHT.*

1. Project cost management deals with all the following EXCEPT: 1.____
   A. Estimating costs
   B. Budgeting
   C. Controlling costs
   D. Communicating costs

2. Which of the following is not a process associated with project cost management? 2.____
   A. Control costs
   B. Maintain reserves
   C. Estimate costs
   D. Determine budget

3. _____ is not a key deliverable of project cost processes. 3.____
   A. Cost performance baseline
   B. Activity cost estimates
   C. Results of estimates
   D. Work performance measurements

4. As a project manager, you are calculating depreciation for an object. You are doing this by depreciating the same amount from the cost each year. What kind of depreciation technique are you applying? 4.____
   A. Sum of year depreciation
   B. Double-declining balance
   C. Multiple depreciation
   D. Straight line depreciation

5. Which of the following is not a characteristic of analogous estimating? 5.____
   A. It is a top-down approach
   B. It is a form of an expert judgment
   C. It makes less time when compared to bottom-up estimation
   D. It is more accurate when compared to bottom-up estimation

6. CPI = EV/AC. If CPI is less than 1, the project 6.____
   A. is over the budget
   B. is within the budget
   C. would be left over with unused budget
   D. efficiency is less

7. Which of the following is not a tool used for estimating cost? 7.____
   A. Cost of quality
   B. Expert judgment
   C. Two point estimates
   D. Three point estimates

8. What are the traditional project management triple constraints? 8.____
   A. Time, cost, resources
   B. Scope, cost, resources
   C. Scope, time, cost
   D. Resources, scope, budget

9. Sam, an IT project manager, is having difficulty getting resources for his project, and hence has to depend highly on department heads.
   Which type of organization is Sam most likely working with?
   A. Functional
   B. Tight Matrix
   C. Weak Matrix
   D. Projectized

10. After-project costs are called _____.
    A. cost of quality
    B. extra costs
    C. life cycle costs
    D. over budget costs

11. Critical chain is a tool and technique for _____.
    A. developing schedule process
    B. defining critical path
    C. sequencing activities process
    D. estimating activity duration

12. The following are outputs for sequencing activities:
    A. Project schedule network diagram, Milestone list
    B. Project document updates, Project schedule network diagram
    C. Project schedule, Project document updates
    D. Schedule data, Schedule baseline

13. The schedule performance index is a measure of:
    A. Difference between earned value and planned value
    B. Ratio between earned value and planned value
    C. Difference between earned value and estimate at completion
    D. Ratio between estimate at completion and earned value

14. Which of the following is not an input, output or tools and technique for control schedule process?
    A. Project schedule, work performance measurements and variance analysis
    B. Project management plan, project document updates and schedule compression
    C. Work performance information, schedule baseline and schedule data
    D. Project schedule, change requests and resource leveling

15. Contracts, resource calendar, risk register and forecasts are all termed as
    A. inputs to administer procurements process
    B. outputs from close procurements process
    C. project documents
    D. tools and techniques of conduct procurement process

16. Fast tracking can be best described as
    A. one of the schedule compression techniques
    B. adding resources to activities on critical path
    C. shared or critical resources available only at specific times
    D. performing activities in parallel to shorten project duration

17. Which of the following contract types places the highest risk on the seller?
    A. Cost plus fixed fee
    B. Firm fixed price
    C. Cost plus incentive fee
    D. Time and material

18. Using the Power/Interest grid, a stakeholder with low power and having high interest on the project should be
    A. monitored
    B. managed closely
    C. kept satisfied
    D. kept informed

19. Stakeholder classification information is found in which of the following documents?
    A. Communications management plan
    B. Stakeholder register
    C. Stakeholder management strategy document
    D. Human resource plan

20. Thomas is a project manager of a well-reputed organization. One of your senior managers approaches you to explain constraints on labor utilization followed by a request to delay a couple of your projects. What is the best way to approach this situation?
    A. Agree with the senior manager and delay a couple of your projects
    B. Perform an impact analysis of the requested change
    C. Report the situation to the senior management and make a complaint against the senior manager
    D. Disagree with the senior manager and continue with the progress of the projects managed by you

21. Project management is defined as
    A. completion of a project
    B. gaining trust of the people involved in the project
    C. completing a WBS
    D. the application of specific knowledge, skills and tools

22. The most common form of dependency is
    A. Start to Start
    B. Finish to Start
    C. Finish to Finish
    D. Start to Finish

23. Kelly is a project manager who is in phase of project evaluation. Which of the following has to be considered during project evaluation phase?
    I.   Give feedback to team members
    II. Learn from experiences
    III. Monitor
    IV. Celebrate

The correct answer(s) is/are:
A. I only
B. I, IV and III
C. III only
D. I, II and IV

24. Which of the following are very vital for the implementation of the project, and also must be repeated over and over during project's life.
    I. Correct
    II. Monitor
    III. Estimate time and cost
    IV. Analyze

    The correct answer(s) is/are:
    A. I, II and III
    B. III only
    C. I, III and IV
    D. I, II and IV

25. What is the average amount of time is to be allocated to project planning?
    A. 10%
    B. 25%
    C. 22%
    D. 2%

KEY (CORRECT ANSWERS)

1. D
2. B
3. C
4. C
5. D

6. A
7. C
8. C
9. A
10. C

11. A
12. B
13. B
14. C
15. C

16. D
17. B
18. D
19. B
20. B

21. D
22. B
23. D
24. D
25. A

TEST 4

DIRECTIONS: Each question or incomplete statement is followed by several suggested answers of completions. Select the one that best answers the question or complete the statement. *PRINT THE LETTER OF THE CORRECT ANSWER IN THE SPACE AT THE RIGHT.*

1. Imagine you are assigned a project for which you do not have the required competency and experience to manage. What is the best plan of action?
    A. Make sure that you disclose any areas of improvement that need to be immediately addressed with the project sponsor before accepting the assignment
    B. Do not inform anyone about the gaps and learn as much as you can before any critical activity is due for delivery
    C. Consider the opportunity as a stepping stone for your career development and accept it
    D. Tell your boss that you cannot manage as you do not have the relevant experience and decline it

1.____

2. You are the project manager of a new project and are involved in selecting a vendor for acquiring products required for the project. Your close friend is running a company that is also very competitive and a reputed one along with other vendors who are competing for the bid. How can you handle this situation?
    A. Do not participate in the vendor selection process as this may be considered a conflict of interest
    B. Provide information to help your friend get the contract as you are the project manager of the project
    C. Do not inform anyone about your personal contact and be involved in the vendor selection process as normal
    D. Discuss with your project sponsor the possibility of a conflict of interest and leave the decision to him on the next steps

2.____

3. You have provided good guidance to your team members and this has resulted in successful execution of all of the phases involved. There was a particular phase that has been identified as very critical and the presence of a technical expert helped achieve this success. In the senior management review meeting you were credited with the success of the project, with specific mention of that particular phase. What do you do in this situation?
    A. Accept the appreciation and feel proud about the success of the project
    B. Do not mention anything about the technical expert role as you were the project manager for this project
    C. Give credit to the technical expert and let the senior management know how the presence of the technical expert helped the team to be successful
    D. Accept the appreciation from the senior management and thank the technical expert in private for achieving this success

3.____

4. As a project manager you are preparing status reports for a meeting with the stakeholders. One of your team members has come out with an issue that will cause some delay in the project timeline. You have a plan that can be implemented to make sure that this issue can be managed without causing any delay in the timeline, but you currently do not have the time to update the project plan. How will you handle this situation?
    A. Present the status of the project as *on-track* without discussing anything about this issue as you will have time to prepare before the next meeting
    B. Cancel the meeting as you do not have the time to update the details to be provided to the stakeholders
    C. Present the status of the project *as-is* without minimizing the effect of the delay and discuss details of the planned approach to solve this issue
    D. Fire your team that is responsible for causing this delay as it has created a bad impression of you amongst the stakeholders

4._____

5. John is an Associate Director in a pharmaceutical company managing its internal projects. He has presented whitepapers on project execution methodologies and is highly respected within the organization. He also regularly conducts workshops & lectures in coordination with PMO. What kind of power does John possess?
    A. Referent power
    B. Coercive power
    C. Reward power
    D. Expert power

5._____

6. You are a project manager working for a non-profit organization. You had been assigned a project that is in the initial stage and involves development of an eco-system in a large community. You are reviewing the deliverables and templates from similar projects that are available in the company lessons learnt knowledge base. Which item will be of much importance to you?
    A. Project Information Management System
    B. Enterprise Environmental Factors
    C. Organization Process Assets
    D. Standard Templates

6._____

7. A project that you were managing is nearing completion. As part of the deliverables you are required to complete lessons-learned documentation of the project. What is the primary purpose of creating lessons-learned documentation?
    A. Provide information of project success
    B. Help identify all the failures
    C. Provide information on minimizing negative impacts and maximizing positive events for future projects of similar nature
    D. Comply with the organization's objectives

7._____

8. You are managing project teams that work from different locations and there has been issues with the teams' ability to effectively perform. This has resulted in delay in timeline. Which kind of team development technique would be most effective in this situation?
    A. Mediation
    B. Training
    C. Co-location
    D. Rewards

8._____

9. The project sponsor has requested that you create a project charter for a new project that you will manage next month. Which document will you utilize to create the project charter that will justify the need for the project?
    A. Project SOW
    B. Business Need
    C. Business Case
    D. Cost-benefit Analysis

9._____

10. An audit is being performed by a team for the project you are managing. The team reports that the standards utilized need to be analyzed as several processes that are not relevant to the current project.
    What is the process that the team is currently involved?
    - A. Quality planning
    - B. Quality control
    - C. Quality assurance
    - D. Benchmark creation

11. The change control board of your organization has approved changes that were submitted and the project team is executing them.
    What would this process be considered?
    - A. Executing the change request
    - B. Implementing a corrective action
    - C. Gold-plating
    - D. Approving the change request

12. Which is the primary technique that is carried out to ensure that a contract award is executed correctly or not?
    - A. Litigation
    - B. Contract negotiation
    - C. Inspections
    - D. Procurement audit

13. In the final stages of completing a project, you and your team are involved in creating the project report that will be presented to the stakeholders. Which of the following information is not appropriate to be included in the final report?
    - A. Recommendations from your team
    - B. Project success factors
    - C. WBS dictionary
    - D. Details of the process improvements

14. At the completion of a project, your team has completed the lessons-learned documentation and archived in the database. Who should have access to these documents?
    - A. Project team members
    - B. Operations department
    - C. All of the company's members
    - D. Functional managers

15. You are project manager for a large project that is in the final stages of completion and you need to formally provide information on the major milestone achieved. You are also in need of immediate feedback from the stakeholders. Which is the best communication method to meet this requirement?
    - A. E-mail
    - B. Web publishing
    - C. Meeting
    - D. Videoconferencing

16. Which document will formally authorize a project manager to start the project?
    - A. Project SOW
    - B. Project Charter
    - C. Business Case
    - D. Stakeholder Register

17. Which of the following documents would be utilized to ascertain the project's investment worthiness?
    - A. Project Charter
    - B. Business Case
    - C. Business Need
    - D. Procurement documents

18. Which of the following conflict resolution is considered as Lose-lose solution?
    A. Problem-solving
    B. Forcing
    C. Compromising
    D. Withdrawing

19. McGregor's Theory states that all workers fit into one of the two groups. Which of the following theories believes that people are willing to work on their own and need less supervision?
    A. Theory X
    B. Theory Y
    C. Maslow's Hierarchy
    D. Expectancy

20. The major cause for conflicts on a project are schedule, project priorities and _____.
    A. cost
    B. resources
    C. personality
    D. management

21. The project manager is responsible for
    A. the success of the project
    B. achieving the project objectives
    C. authorizing the project
    D. performing the project work

22. Which of the following actions correspond to reducing the consequences of future problems?
    A. Corrective action
    B. Preventive action
    C. Defect repair
    D. Change request

23. As a project manager for a large-scale project, you are in the process of procuring materials required for the project. Which of the following documents will you not be responsible for?
    A. Procurement documents
    B. Procurement statements of work
    C. Source selection criteria
    D. Proposals

24. During which process group will the detailed requirements be gathered?
    A. Initiating
    B. Planning
    C. Executing
    D. Closing

25. The values that illustrate PMIs code of ethics and professional conduct are
    A. respect, honesty, responsibility and honorability
    B. honesty, cultural diversity, integrity and responsibility
    C. fairness, responsibility, honesty and respect
    D. honorability, fairness, respect and responsibility

KEY (CORRECT ANSWERS)

1. A
2. D
3. C
4. C
5. D

6. C
7. C
8. C
9. C
10. C

11. A
12. D
13. C
14. C
15. D

16. B
17. B
18. C
19. B
20. B

21. B
22. B
23. D
24. B
25. C

EXAMINATION SECTION
TEST 1

DIRECTIONS: Each question or incomplete statement is followed by several suggested answers of completions. Select the one that BEST answers the question or Complete the statement. *PRINT THE LETTER OF THE CORRECT ANSWER IN THE SPACE AT THE RIGHT.*

1. An accepted deadline for a project approaches. However, the project manager realizes only 85% of the work has been completed. The project manager then issues a change request.
   What should the change request authorize?

   A. Corrective action based on causes
   B. Escalation approval to use contingency funding
   C. Additional resources using the contingency fund
   D. Team overtime to meet schedule

2. _____ is a valid tool or technique to assist the project manager to assure the success of the process improvement plan.

   A. Benchmarking
   B. Change control system
   C. Process analysis
   D. Configuration management system

3. A project manager meets with the project team to review lessons learned from previous projects. In what activity is the team involved?

   A. Performance management
   B. Project team status meeting
   C. Scope identification
   D. Risk identification

4. _____ process helps you to purchase goods from external suppliers.

   A. Quality management
   B. Procurement management
   C. Cost management
   D. Communication management

5. Which of the following is not involved in procurement management?

   A. Review supplier performance against contract
   B. Identify and resolve supplier performance issues
   C. Communicate the status to management
   D. Manage a WBS

6. _____ contract is advantageous to a buyer.

   A. Fixed price
   B. Cost reimbursable
   C. Time and material
   D. Fixed price plus incentive

7. Which of the following contracts is advantageous to a seller?

    A. Fixed price
    B. Cost reimbursable
    C. Time and material
    D. Fixed price plus incentive

8. Tom is a manager of a project whose deliverable has many uncertainties associated with it. What kind of contract should he use during the procurement process?

    A. Fixed price
    B. Cost reimbursable
    C. Time and material
    D. Fixed price plus incentive

9. Cost plus _____ is not a cost-reimbursable contract.

    A. fixed fee
    B. fee
    C. fixed time
    D. incentive fee

10. _____ type of contract helps both the seller and buyer to save, if the performance criteria are exceeded.

    A. Cost plus fixed fee
    B. Cost plus fee
    C. Cost plus fixed time
    D. Cost plus incentive fee

11. A project manager with a construction company. She has to complete a project in a specified time, but does have enough time to send the job out for bids. What type of contract would save her time?

    A. Fixed price
    B. Cost reimbursable
    C. Time and material
    D. Fixed price plus incentive

12. The major type(s) of standard warranty (ies) that are used in the business environment is (are):

    A. express
    B. negotiated
    C. implied
    D. A and C

13. During contract management, the project manager must consider the

    A. acquisition process and contract administration
    B. contract administration and ecological environment
    C. ecological environment and acquisition process
    D. offer, acceptance and consideration

14. Which contract type places the most risk on the seller? 14._____

    A. Cost plus percentage fee
    B. Cost plus incentive fee
    C. Cost plus fixed fee
    D. Firm fixed price

15. Finalizing project close-out happens when a project manager 15._____

    A. archives the project records
    B. completes the contract
    C. complete lessons learned
    D. reassigns the team

16. Unit price contract is fair to both owner and contractor, 16._____

    A. as the actual volumes will be measured and paid as the work proceeds
    B. as the owner will provide bill of quantities
    C. as both are absorbing an equal amount of risk
    D. all of the above

17. Bill is the manager of a project that requires different areas of expertise. 17._____
    Which one of the following contracts should he sign?

    A. Fixed price
    B. Cost reimbursable
    C. Time and material
    D. Unit price

18. Which of the following contracts is commonly used in projects that involve pilot 18._____
    programs or harness new technologies?

    A. Fixed price
    B. Incentive
    C. Time and material
    D. Unit price

19. Procurement cycle involves all of the following steps EXCEPT 19._____

    A. supplier contract
    B. renewal
    C. sending a proposal
    D. information gathering

20. What would happen if a project manager does not take up a background review during the 20._____
    procurement process?

    A. Price might not be negotiated
    B. Credibility of the goods might not be validated
    C. Goods might not be shipped
    D. Both A and B

21. _____ is not a part of a procurement document.   21._____

    A. Buyer's commencement to the bid
    B. Summons by the financially responsible party
    C. Establishing terms and conditions of a contract
    D. Roles of responsibilities of internal team

22. Which of the following is NOT an example of a procurement document?   22._____

    A. Offers
    B. Contracts
    C. Project record archives
    D. Request for quotation

23. A project manager needs to follow _____ for a good procurement   23._____
    document to be drafted.

    A. clear definition of the responsibilities, rights and commitments of both parties
       in the contract
    B. clear definition of the nature and quality of the goods or services to be provided
    C. clear and easy to understand language
    D. all of the above

24. Which of the following is not a concern with respect to procurement management?   24._____

    A. Reassigning the team
    B. Not all goods and services that a business requires need to be purchased from
       outside
    C. You would need to have a good idea of what you exactly require and then go
       on to consider various options and alternatives
    D. You would need to consider different criteria, apart from just the cost, to finally
       decide on which supplier you would want to go with.

25. Source qualifications are a part of the _____ phase of Acquisition Process Cycle.   25._____

    A. post-award
    B. pre-award
    C. award
    D. origination

KEY (CORRECT ANSWERS)

1. A
2. C
3. D
4. B
5. D

6. A
7. B
8. B
9. C
10. D

11. C
12. D
13. A
14. D
15. B

16. C
17. D
18. B
19. C
20. B

21. D
22. C
23. D
24. A
25. C

TEST 2

DIRECTIONS: Each question or incomplete statement is followed by several suggested answers of completions. Select the one that BEST answers the question or Complete the statement. *PRINT THE LETTER OF THE CORRECT ANSWER IN THE SPACE AT THE RIGHT.*

1. Which of the following project tools details the project scope? 1.____

    A. Project plan
    B. Gantt chart
    C. Milestone checklist
    D. Score cards

2. Which of the following is NOT a project tool? 2.____

    A. Gantt chart
    B. Milestone checklist
    C. Score cards
    D. MS project

3. _____ is accompanied by project audits by a third party. As a result, non-compliance and action items are tracked. 3.____

    A. Gantt chart
    B. Milestone checklist
    C. Project reviews
    D. Delivery reviews

4. An IT project manager, is involved in tracking his team's performance. Which tool would he use to gauge this performance? 4.____

    A. Score cards
    B. Gantt chart
    C. Project management software
    D. Milestone checklist

5. What tool does a manager use to track the interdependencies of each project activity? 5.____

    A. Project plan
    B. Gantt chart
    C. Project management software
    D. Milestone checklist

6. Which tool would be used for a manager to determine if he or she is on track in terms of project progress? 6.____

    A. Project management software
    B. Delivery reviews
    C. Project reviews
    D. Milestone checklist

7. Which of the following tools is used for individual member promotion?

    A. Delivery reviews
    B. Score cards
    C. Project reviews
    D. Milestone checklist

8. Which of the following is NOT a project management process?

    A. Project planning
    B. Project initiation
    C. Project management software
    D. Closeout and evaluation

9. _____ is the phase in which the service provider proves the eligibility and ability of completing the project to the client.

    A. Pre-sale period
    B. Project execution
    C. Sign-off
    D. Closeout and evaluation

10. Controlling of the project could be done by following all of the following protocols EXCEPT

    A. communication plan
    B. quality assurance test plan
    C. test plan
    D. project plan

11. A manager wants his project to be successful and hence verifies the successful outcome of every activity leading to successful completion of the project. Which of the following activities would he use to do so?

    A. Control
    B. Test plan
    C. Project plan
    D. Validation

12. What happens during the closeout and evaluation phase?

    A. Evaluation of the entire project
    B. Hand over the implemented system
    C. Identifying mistakes and taking necessary action
    D. All of the above

13. A project manager, is conducting validation and verification functions. Which team's assistance would she need in order to do so?

    A. Quality assurance team
    B. Project team
    C. Client team
    D. Third-party vendor

14. Tracking the effort and cost of the project is done during _____.

    A. project execution
    B. control and validation
    C. closeout and evaluation
    D. communication plan

15. _____ is the entity created for governing the processes, practices, tools and other activities related to project management in an organization.

    A. Project management office
    B. Project management software
    C. Quality assurance
    D. None of the above

16. A project management office must be built with the following considerations EXCEPT

    A. process optimization
    B. productivity enhancement
    C. building the bottom line of their organization
    D. none of the above

17. An advantage of a project management office is that it

    A. helps cut down staff
    B. helps cut down resources
    C. refines the processes related to project management
    D. all of the above

18. A project management office could fail because of

    A. lack of executive management support
    B. incapability
    C. it adds figures to the bottom line of the company
    D. both A and B

19. _____ is used to analyze the difficulties that may arise due to the execution of the project.

    A. Project management office
    B. Project management triangle
    C. Both A and B
    D. None of the above

20. The three constraints in a project management triangle are _____.

    A. time, cost and scope
    B. time, resources and quality
    C. time, resources and people
    D. time, resources and cost

21. A project manager, is experiencing challenges related to project triangle and hence finds difficulty in achieving the project objectives. Which of the following skills would help her?   21._____

    A. Time management
    B. Effective communication
    C. Managing people
    D. All of the above

22. _____ is NOT a role of a project manager.   22._____

    A. Carrying out basic project tasks
    B. Keeping stakeholders informed on the project progress
    C. Defining project scope and assigning tasks to team members
    D. Setting objectives

23. Kathy is advising Nicole on the goals and challenges a project manager must consider. Which of the following should she discuss?   23._____

    A. Deadlines
    B. Client satisfaction
    C. No budget overrun
    D. All of the above

24. Team management deals with all of the following EXCEPT   24._____

    A. providing incentives and encouragement
    B. maintaining warm and friendly relationship with teammates
    C. meeting requirements of the client
    D. including them in project related decisions

25. _____ is vital to win client satisfaction.   25._____

    A. Finishing the work on scheduled time
    B. Ensuring that most standards are met
    C. Having a limited relationship with the client
    D. All of the above

KEY (CORRECT ANSWERS)

1. A
2. D
3. C
4. A
5. B

6. D
7. B
8. C
9. A
10. C

11. D
12. D
13. A
14. A
15. A

16. D
17. C
18. D
19. B
20. A

21. D
22. A
23. D
24. C
25. A

TEST 3

DIRECTIONS: Each question or incomplete statement is followed by several suggested answers of completions. Select the one that BEST answers the question or Complete the statement. *PRINT THE LETTER OF THE CORRECT ANSWER IN THE SPACE AT THE RIGHT.*

1. What type of strategy is followed by a manager before his workforce focuses on with performance?

    A. Activators
    B. Behaviors
    C. Consequences
    D. Deviators

    1._____

2. _____ define how the workforce performs or behaves within the activity or situation as a result of activators or consequences.

    A. Deviators
    B. Consequences
    C. Behaviors
    D. Activators

    2._____

3. _____ explain how the manager handles the workforce after the performance.

    A. Deviators
    B. Consequences
    C. Behaviors
    D. Activators

    3._____

4. Which of the following is found to have a great impact on workforce behavior?

    A. Deviators
    B. Consequences
    C. Behaviors
    D. Activators

    4._____

5. Nancy, an IT project manager, is keen to delegate her work. She is aware that a good manager's role is about delegating work effectively in order to complete the task. What should she consider before delegating?

    A. Delegating the work with clear instructions and expectations stated
    B. Providing enough moral support
    C. Identify individuals that are capable of carrying out a particular task
    D. All the above

    5._____

6. Which of the following is NOT a tool related to controlling and assuring quality?

    A. Check sheet
    B. Cause-and-effect diagram
    C. Activators
    D. Scatter diagram

    6._____

7. _____ are used for understanding business, implementation and organizational problems.

    A. Cause-and-effect diagrams
    B. Scatter diagrams
    C. Control charts
    D. Pareto charts

    7._____

8. Jim is replacing the earlier project manager in the middle of the project and hard-pressed with time. He has to work on a priority basis.
   Which of the following tools would he use to identify priorities?

   A. Cause-and-effect diagram
   B. Scatter diagram
   C. Control chart
   D. Pareto chart

Questions 9-11 refer to the following chart.

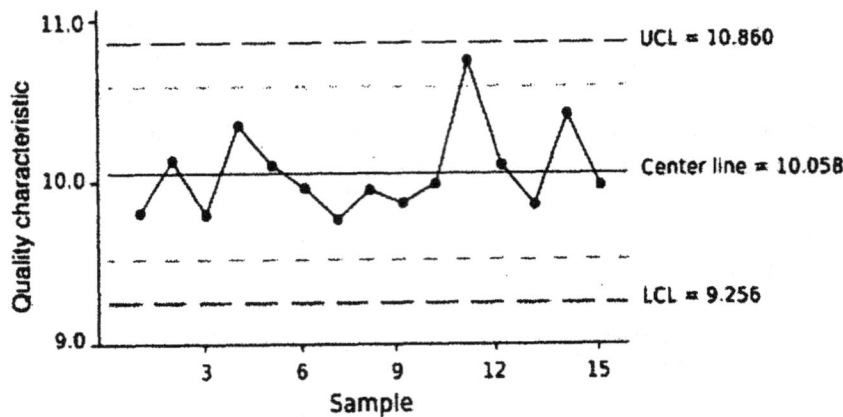

9. What type of tool is this?

   A. Control chart
   B. Flow chart
   C. Scatter diagram
   D. Pareto chart

10. The above-mentioned chart/tool is used for _____.

    A. identifying sets of priorities
    B. comparing two variables
    C. monitoring the performance of a process
    D. gathering and organizing data

11. The above chart/tool could be used to identify all of the following EXCEPT

    A. the stability of the process
    B. the common cause of variation
    C. the parameter(s) that have the highest impact on the specific concern
    D. conditions where the monitoring team needs to react

12. Which of the following tools would a project manager use to perform a trend analysis?

    A. Flow chart
    B. Scatter diagram
    C. Cause-and-effect diagram
    D. Pareto chart

13. _____ is/are a common and simple method used by project managers to arrive at an effective cause-and-effect diagram.

    A. Survey
    B. Brainstorming
    C. Informal discussions
    D. Formal presentations

14. Which of the following tools should a project manager use to gain a brief understanding of the project's critical path?

    A. Flow chart
    B. Pareto chart
    C. Histogram
    D. Check sheet

15. _____ is NOT a step involved in the benchmarking process.

    A. Planning
    B. Analysis of data
    C. Monitoring
    D. None of the above

16. As a project manager, where will you collect primary data when you collect information?

    i) Benchmarked company
    ii) Press
    iii) Publication
    iv) Website

    A. Only I
    B. Both I and II
    C. I, II, III and IV
    D. Both I and IV

17. Which of the following methods is recommended to conduct primary research?

    A. E-mail
    B. Referring to the website of other companies
    C. Telephone
    D. Face-to-face interviews

18. Analysis of data involves all of the following EXCEPT

    A. sharing data with all the stakeholders
    B. data presentation
    C. results projection
    D. classifying the performance gaps in processes

19. _____ is referred to as an enabler, which will help project managers to act wisely.

    A. Projection of results
    B. Performance gap identification
    C. Root cause of performance gaps
    D. Presentation of data

20. Which of the following needs to be done in order to monitor the quality of the project?

    A. Evaluating the progress made
    B. Reiterating the impact of change
    C. Making necessary adjustments
    D. All the above

Use the following cause-and-effect diagram to answer questions 21 through 23.

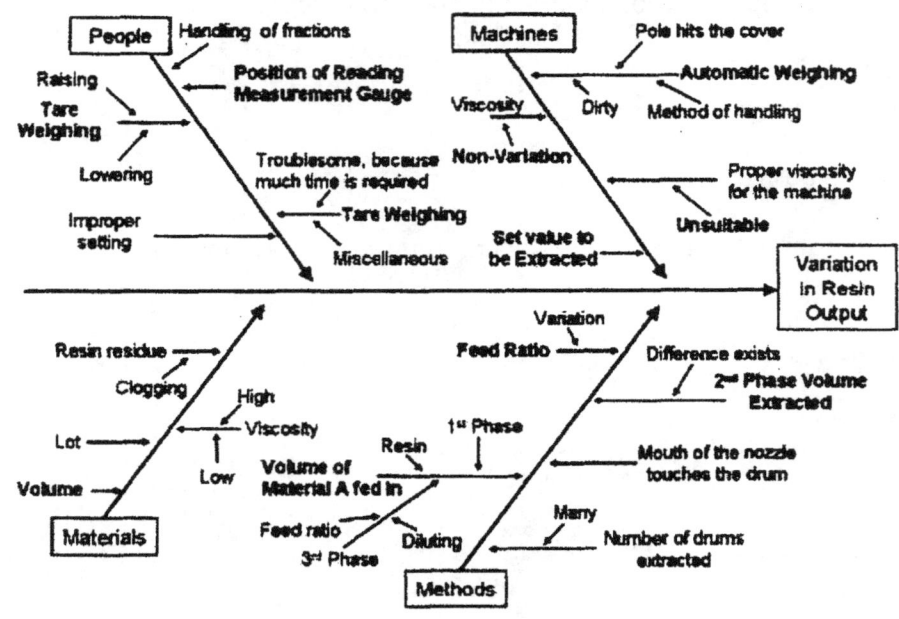

21. Which of the following is NOT represented in this diagram?

    A. Problem
    B. Major cause of the problem
    C. Contributing factors
    D. Possible causes of the problem

22. What is the effect with respect to the diagram?

    A. Materials
    B. Methods
    C. Variation in Resin Output
    D. People

23. As a project manager, what will you do to gain a better understanding of the problems and handling them?

    A. Investigations
    B. Surveys
    C. Interviews
    D. All the above

24. Kotter's change management process involves all the following steps EXCEPT

    A. building a team
    B. resource management
    C. creating a vision
    D. removing obstacles

25. _____ lets team members know why they are working on a change initiative.

    A. Removing obstacles
    B. Building a team
    C. Integrating the change
    D. Creating a vision

KEY (CORRECT ANSWERS)

1. A
2. C
3. B
4. B
5. D

6. C
7. A
8. D
9. A
10. C

11. C
12. B
13. B
14. A
15. D

16. C
17. B
18. A
19. C
20. D

21. B
22. C
23. D
24. B
25. D

TEST 4

DIRECTIONS: Each question or incomplete statement is followed by several suggested answers of completions. Select the one that best answers the question or Complete the statement. *PRINT THE LETTER OF THE CORRECT ANSWER IN THE SPACE AT THE RIGHT.*

1. Which of the following is NOT a communication blocker?
    A. Judging
    B. Accusing
    C. Globalizing
    D. Listening

    1._____

2. Using words like "always" and "never" is an example of _____.
    A. judging
    B. accusing
    C. globalizing
    D. listening

    2._____

3. What should you do as a project manager to eliminate communication blockers?
    A. Encourage others to avoid communication blockers by educating them
    B. Be aware of the various blockers and take steps to remove them
    C. Model to promote effective and empathetic communication
    D. All of the above

    3._____

4. What would happen if there were no proper communication channel?
    A. Inefficient flow of information
    B. Clarity among employees on what is expected of them
    C. Sense of company mind/common vision among employees
    D. Clarity among employees on the happening within the company

    4._____

5. As a project manager, you could use any one of the following types of language EXCEPT _____ for communicating with your team.
    A. formal
    B. insulting
    C. informal
    D. unofficial

    5._____

6. A(n) _____ is/are NOT an example of formal communication.
    A. annual report
    B. business plan
    C. social gathering
    D. review meetings

    6._____

7. _____ types of communication are used to communicate company policies, goals and procedures.
   A. Formal
   B. Informal
   C. Unofficial
   D. None of the above

8. _____ is NOT an example of informal communication.
   A. Survey
   B. Quality circle
   C. Team work
   D. Training program

9. "Grapevine" is an example of _____ communication.
   A. Formal
   B. Informal
   C. Unofficial
   D. None of the above

10. What question would you NOT consider as a project manager before choosing the right method to communicate?
    A. Who is the target audience?
    B. Will it lead to employee productivity?
    C. What kind of information would be helpful for clarity among employees?
    D. Which is the best way to threaten the employees?

11. Which of the following is not included in "The Five Ws of Communication Management"?
    A. What information would prompt employees to work out of fear?
    B. What information is essential for the project?
    C. What is the time required for the communication to happen effectively?
    D. Who requires information and what type of information is required?

12. _____ refers to developing a message.
    A. Decoding
    B. Encoding
    C. Transmission
    D. Feedback

13. _____ refers to interpreting the message.
    A. Decoding
    B. Encoding
    C. Transmission
    D. Feedback

14. Which of the following is not necessarily involved in a communication process?
    A. Sender
    B. Transmission
    C. Vision
    D. Receiver

15. _____ is NOT a sign of active listening.
    A. Making eye contact
    B. Asking questions to gain clarity
    C. Using gestures like nodding head
    D. Using gestures that distract the speaker

16. Madeline is a project manager and involved in conflict management. Which of the following should she use to manage a conflict?
    A. Identify actions that resolve conflicts
    B. Identify actions that would aggravate conflicts
    C. Consider different methods of resolving the conflict
    D. All the above

17. A managerial action that would NOT aggravate conflict is _____.
    A. poor communication
    B. assertive style of leadership
    C. ill-defined expectations
    D. authoritative style of leadership

18. An example of a managerial action that would NOT minimize a conflict is
    A. well-defined job descriptions
    B. participative approach
    C. submissive style of leadership
    D. fostering team spirit

19. Which of the following methods could you use as a project manager to handle conflicts?
    A. Flight
    B. Fake
    C. Fight
    D. All of the above

20. _____ is the term used when people run away from problems instead of confronting them and turn to avoidance as a means of handling conflict.
    A. Flight
    B. Fake
    C. Fight
    D. Fold

21. _____ is the term used when an individual is made to agree to a solution by means of browbeating.
    A. Flight
    B. Fake
    C. Fight
    D. Fold

22. Which of the following is NOT a step in conflict management?
    A. Choose the best solution that satisfy most people most of the time and implement this
    B. Engage in participatory dialogue and find a range of solutions that will be acceptable to all the parties concerned
    C. Eliminate those who promote mutual understanding and acceptance
    D. Identify the limiting resource or constraint that is generally at the root cause of the conflict

23. Which of the following is NOT a skill required for conflict resolution?
    A. Clarity in communication
    B. Aggressiveness
    C. Negotiation
    D. Listening

24. _____ is essential to be prepared for any problems that may arise when it is least expected.
    A. Conflict management
    B. Communication management
    C. Crisis management
    D. None of the above

25. Which of the following is NOT a type of crisis?   25._____
    A. Financial
    B. Technological
    C. Natural
    D. Negotiation

KEY (CORRECT ANSWERS)

1. D	11. A
2. C	12. B
3. D	13. A
4. A	14. C
5. B	15. D
6. C	16. D
7. A	17. B
8. A	18. C
9. C	19. D
10. D	20. A

21. D
22. C
23. B
24. C
25. D

EXAMINATION SECTION
TEST 1

DIRECTIONS: Each question or incomplete statement is followed by several suggested answers of completions. Select the one that best answers the question or Complete the statement. *PRINT THE LETTER OF THE CORRECT ANSWER IN THE SPACE AT THE RIGHT.*

1. In the OSI model, a hub is defined in which of the following layers? 1._____

    A. Session
    B. Application
    C. Data link
    D. Physical

2. A simple definition of bandwidth is the 2._____

    A. number of computers in a network
    B. transmission capacity
    C. classification of network IPs
    D. none of the above

3. _____ topology makes use of terminators. 3._____

    A. Star
    B. Ring
    C. Bus
    D. Token ring

4. Which of the following is an advantage of the use of multimedia in the learning process? 4._____

    A. Students can express their abilities in many different ways
    B. It is useful for the students to develop their career in media sciences
    C. It enhances students' motivation for learning
    D. None of the above

5. For the purpose of transfer of technology, companies/organizations must 5._____

    A. allocate much better budget for research and development
    B. have a good networking structure
    C. have willingness to spend on technology to gain long-term benefits
    D. all of the above

6. The focus of teacher education must be on the development of 6._____

    A. professional identity
    B. personal identity
    C. academic identity
    D. none of the above

7. System Study is a study that 7._____

    A. studies an existing system
    B. performs the documentation of the existing system
    C. highlights existing deficiencies and establishes new goals
    D. all of the above

8. Which of these is the starting point for the establishment of an MIS?

    A. Development of physical hardware and networking structure
    B. Development of a DBMS
    C. Understanding and identification of business processes
    D. None of the above

9. A new system is designed by the system analyst by

    A. identifying the subsystems and then creating links among these subsystems
    B. customizing an existing system to the new system
    C. creating a one unit larger system
    D. proposing new system alternatives

10. Process mapping may be defined by which of the following?

    A. Activities are related to the different functional units of the organization
    B. It is developed by the placement of different activities with the help of symbols in a logical order
    A. It is used to present different activities of a process in a hierarchical form
    B. Process efficiency is measured with the help of process mapping

11. Which of the following is an example of a payment system?

    A. E-commerce shopping
    B. Travel reimbursement
    C. Accounts payable
    D. All of the above

12. _____ phase performs problem analysis.

    A. Systems Analysis
    B. System Design
    C. System Implementation
    D. None of the above

13. Top management is most concerned with

    A. daily transactions
    B. strategic decisions
    C. tactical decisions
    D. both (B) and (C)

14. Most companies and organizations have their _____ MIS plans.

    A. master
    B. broad
    C. prototype
    D. control

15. Data integrity refers to

    A. simplicity
    B. security
    C. validity
    D. none of the above

16. The desired outcome for project integration is

    A. better focus on the organization
    B. ideal usage of resources of the organization
    C. better communication among projects and their teams
    D. all of the above

17. If you are working on more than one project and you frequently need to put work on one project on hold and move to another project, then return later to the original project, this is known as

    A. excessive burden
    B. flexible Processing
    C. multitasking
    D. burnout

18. Which of the following may be defined as a project aim?

    A. Meeting the specific quality requirements
    B. On-time delivery
    C. Working within budget constraints
    D. All of the above

19. The progressive phases of management over large projects are best described as

    A. planning, evaluating and scheduling
    B. planning, scheduling and operating
    C. scheduling, planning and operating
    D. planning, scheduling and controlling

20. Variance of the total project completion time is computed in the PERT analysis as

    A. project final activity variance
    B. the aggregation of variances of the project activities
    C. the aggregation of all the activities variance on the critical path
    D. the aggregation of all the activities variance not on the critical path

21. What will be critical path standard deviation if there are three activities -- X, Y and Z -- in the path? X has a deviation of 2, Y has a deviation of 1 and there is a deviation of 2 for Z. In this case, what is the standard deviation of critical path?

    A. 20
    B. 3
    C. 12
    D. 5

22. Linear regression is much similar to

    A. simple moving average forecasting approach
    B. trend project forecasting approach
    C. weighted moving average forecasting approach
    D. naïve forecasting approach

23. The purpose of risk tolerance is to

    A. observe that how much risk can be tolerated by the project
    B. rank project risks
    C. help the project manager in project estimation
    D. help in project scheduling

24. The process group for project management is ordered

    A. initiating, planning, executing, controlling, and closeout
    B. starting, planning, accelerating, and control
    C. planning, establishing, developing, and control
    D. none of the above

25. Which risk management process identifies the workaround?

    A. Risk identification
    B. Risk monitoring
    C. Risk measurement
    D. Risk monitoring and control

KEY (CORRECT ANSWERS)

1. D	11. D
2. B	12. A
3. C	13. B
4. C	14. A
5. D	15. C
6. A	16. C
7. D	17. C
8. C	18. D
9. A	19. D
10. A	20. C

21. B
22. B
23. B
24. A
25. D

TEST 2

DIRECTIONS: Each question or incomplete statement is followed by several suggested answers of completions. Select the one that best answers the question or Complete the statement. *PRINT THE LETTER OF THE CORRECT ANSWER IN THE SPACE AT THE RIGHT.*

1. What is a computer network? 1._____

    A. Information and resource sharing
    B. A combination of computer systems and other hardware elements
    C. A network of communication channels
    D. All of above

2. A network bridge _____. 2._____

    A. monitors network traffic
    B. distinguishes LANs
    C. is a source of connection among LANs
    D. none of the above

3. Which topology is best for the larger networks? 3._____

    A. Ring token
    B. Star
    C. Ring
    D. Bus

4. Interactive books are used in the form of 4._____

    A. educational games
    B. interactive storybooks
    C. interactive texts
    D. both B and C

5. Which of the following are used for GSM technology? 5._____

    A. OFDMA
    B. FDMA/TDMA
    C. CDMA
    D. None of the above

6. What is the main objective of a MIS department? 6._____

    A. To aid the other business areas in performing their tasks
    B. Information processing for the better utilization of data
    C. To be useful for chief executives
    D. To generate useful information

7. Documentation is prepared at 7._____

    A. every phase
    B. the system analysis phase
    C. the system design phase
    D. the system implementation phase

8. System prototyping is useful for the

   A. programmer in regards to understanding the whole system
   B. purpose of communication with the users, telling them how the system will look after development
   A. purpose of system demo to the higher project management
   B. Both A and B

9. Mistakes made during the requirements analysis phase normally show up in

   A. system design
   B. system testing
   C. system implementation
   D. none of the above

10. Use case analysis is best described by which of the following statements?

    A. It is used for interface design by highlighting the stages of user interaction with the system
    A. It minimizes the number of steps in order to access the content
    B. A consistent site design with the products and services
    C. It is used for the purpose of information categorization

11. Who is responsible for the analysis and design of the systems?

    A. Developer
    B. System analyst
    C. System operator
    D. Project manager

12. _____ is an outline for the development of bugs-free information systems.

    A. System development life cycle
    B. System conversion
    C. Case tools
    D. System analysis

13. Top-down analysis and design is performed by

    A. the creation of system flow chart after design process
    B. identifying the top-level functions and development of subsequent lower-level components
    C. identifying the root elements and then moving gradually up to the top level
    D. none of the above

14. Which of the following is not the part of marketing mix?

    A. Place
    B. Product
    C. Part
    D. Promotion

15. A distributed MIS mainly deals with the

    A. local data processing
    B. multiprocessing
    C. sharing of workload
    D. all of the above

16. Project managers unaware of the importance of a project for the organization might tend to

    A. focus on less important things
    B. emphasize too much on the use of technology
    C. concentrate more on the customer in hand
    D. all of the above

17. Why is it necessary for the project managers to understand the organization's mission?

    A. To make better decisions and required adjustments
    B. To advocate for projects in a better way
    C. In order to perform their jobs more effectively
    D. Both (A) and (B) are correct

18. Common multi-criteria selection models include

    A. checklist
    B. NPV
    C. weighted criteria model
    D. both A and C

19. The project management process does not involve

    A. project scheduling
    B. project planning
    C. system analysis
    D. project estimation

20. Which of the following is the best tool for monitoring projects against the original plan?

    A. Network diagrams
    B. Gantt Charts
    C. Data Flow diagrams
    D. All of the above

21. A project can be treated as a failed project if

    A. project requirements are met on schedule
    B. the project is completed on time but with flaws that require additional work
    C. costs are in line with original projections
    D. all of the above

22. Which of the following is a basic assumption of PERT?

    A. There is no repetition of any activity within the network
    B. There is known time for the completion of each activity
    C. Only the activities in the critical path must be performed
    D. Project start to project end contains only one route

23. Sharing of confidential information with some bidders with the purpose of providing them some undue favor is considered as

    A. bribery
    B. bid rigging
    C. bid fixing
    D. favoritism

24. The advantages of centralized contracting include

    A. provision of easier access to contracting expertise
    B. enhanced organizational contracting expertise
    C. higher level of loyalty
    D. none of the above

25. All of the following are features and characteristics of a project EXCEPT

    A. a defined start and end
    B. a network of related activities
    C. repeated at a regular interval
    D. temporary in nature

KEY (CORRECT ANSWERS)

1. D	11. B
2. C	12. A
3. B	13. B
4. D	14. C
5. B	15. C
6. A	16. D
7. A	17. D
8. B	18. D
9. C	19. C
10. A	20. B

21. B
22. A
23. B
24. B
25. C

TEST 3

DIRECTIONS: Each question or incomplete statement is followed by several suggested answers of completions. Select the one that best answers the question or Complete the statement. *PRINT THE LETTER OF THE CORRECT ANSWER IN THE SPACE AT THE RIGHT.*

1. The number of layers in the OSI Reference Model are

   A. 5
   B. 6
   C. 7
   D. 8

   1._____

2. Which of these is a source of connection oriented message communication?

   A. TCP
   B. UDP
   C. IP
   D. None of the above

   2._____

3. Which buffer is used by the print server for the holding of data before printing?

   A. Node
   B. Spool
   C. Queue
   D. None of above

   3._____

4. Criteria for evaluating commercial hypermedia products include

   A. instructional design
   B. low cost
   C. portability
   D. use of all media channels

   4._____

5. The domain of .net is used by

   A. universities
   B. internet service providers
   C. government organizations
   D. none of the above

   5._____

6. Which of the following is a technology used for the routing of phone calls over a network?

   A. Video-conferencing
   B. VOIP
   C. Teleconferencing
   D. None of the above

   6._____

7. The maintenance phase

   A. defines system requirements
   B. develops system design
   C. performs system testing
   D. none of the above

   7._____

8. Reconstruction of a system requires the consideration of

   A. system inputs and outputs
   B. control and processors
   C. comprehensive user feedback
   D. all of the above

9. Cost-Benefit analysis

   A. performs an estimation of the cost of hardware and software
   B. performs a comparison of costs with the benefits of development of new system
   C. considers both the tangible and non-tangible elements
   D. all of the above

10. Who is responsible for the sponsoring and funding of the project development and its maintenance?

    A. System manager
    B. Project manager
    C. Systems owner
    D. External system user

11. The system implementation approach used in the event you want to run both the old and new systems is called

    A. parallel
    B. pilot
    C. synchronized
    D. phased

12. DBMS advantages include

    A. data integrity
    B. minimization of storage space
    C. centralized access to the data
    D. all of the above

13. Which of the following is a well-known and popular forecasting approach?

    A. Chi Square
    B. Correlation
    C. Regression Analysis
    D. None of the above

14. Who is responsible for the tactical decisions of allocation of resources and establishment of control over project activities?

    A. Middle-level management
    B. Higher-level management
    C. Lower-level management
    D. All of the above

15. The mission statement of an organization answers which of the following questions? 15.____

    A. How do we utilize resources?
    B. What are our goals and intentions as an organization?
    C. What are our plans in the long run?
    D. What is the mode of operations in the current environment?

16. What is the benefit of network approach? 16.____

    A. Forecasts may be carried on
    B. Structured approach is avoided
    C. Project progress against the original plan can be monitored
    D. Requirement of management judgment is eliminated

17. A Gantt chart is composed of 17.____

    A. activities in a sequence
    B. mention of different project activities with the elapsed time
    C. overall project elapsed time
    D. all of the above

18. What does *slack* mean with reference to PERT and CPM? 18.____

    A. It is the latest time on which a project may be started without causing any delay for the project
    B. It is a task which must be completed
    C. This reflects the amount of time a specific task may be delayed without having a need to change the overall time of completion of the project
    D. It reflects the start and end time of a task

19. The direct responsibilities of the project manager include 19.____

    A. calculation of probability of the task's completion
    B. design of the network diagrams
    C. acting on all aspects of the project
    D. ensuring that all people assigned to a project carry out their required duties and utilize appropriate resources and information in order to perform their tasks

20. What is standard error in a regression forecast? 20.____

    A. The highest error level for the forecast
    B. The regression line variability
    C. Time to be consumed for the computation of regression forecast
    D. Forecast validity time

21. Which management process helps in risk identification? 21.____

    A. Risk identification, monitoring and control
    B. Qualitative risk analysis
    C. Quantitative risk analysis
    D. Risk detection

22. The cost reimbursable contracts are termed as _____ contracts.

    A. gradual payment
    B. cost plus
    C. back charge
    D. secure cost

23. The style of conflict resolution that typically has the best impact is

    A. empathy
    B. problem solving
    C. willingness
    D. mapping

24. Decomposition of deliverables into more manageable components is termed as

    A. scope segmentation
    B. scope certification
    C. scoping
    D. scope definition

25. What is quality?

    A. The level at which project requirements are met
    B. Providing output beyond customer demand
    C. Meeting the objectives of management
    D. Meeting customer demands

KEY (CORRECT ANSWERS)

1. C
2. A
3. B
4. A
5. B

6. B
7. D
8. D
9. D
10. C

11. A
12. D
13. C
14. A
15. B

16. C
17. D
18. C
19. D
20. B

21. A
22. B
23. B
24. D
25. A

TEST 4

DIRECTIONS: Each question or incomplete statement is followed by several suggested answers of completions. Select the one that best answers the question or Complete the statement. *PRINT THE LETTER OF THE CORRECT ANSWER IN THE SPACE AT THE RIGHT.*

1. A firewall is a

    A. tool for web browsing
    B. network boundary established physically
    C. system that blocks unauthorized access
    D. computer's network

    1._____

2. For data transfer in both directions, which communication approach is utilized?

    A. Simplex
    B. Half duplex
    C. Full duplex
    D. None of the above

    2._____

3. Which of the following is utilized for the purpose of modulation and demodulation?

    A. Satellite
    B. Fiber optics
    C. Modem
    D. Coaxial Cable

    3._____

4. After looking at the header of the data packet, a _____ decides the destination of the packet.

    A. hub
    B. switch
    C. router
    D. firewall

    4._____

5. Which of the following is software for video editing?

    A. iMovie
    B. ScanImage
    C. PhotoShop
    D. HyperStudio

    5._____

6. The use of educational technology must be considered as a(n)

    A. alternative to less technological strategies
    B. necessity for learning
    C. supplement to other teaching tools
    D. none the above

    6._____

7. Parallel Run refers to

    A. job processing of two different tasks at two different terminals to compare the outputs
    B. concurrent running of old and new systems in order to identify the likely mistakes of the new system and to perform the daily routine tasks
    C. a job run at two different systems for the purpose of speed comparison
    D. all of the above

    7._____

8. The purpose of a context diagram is to

   A. establish system context
   B. present the flow of data of the system in order to provide a broader system overview
   C. provide a detailed system description
   D. none of the above

9. The number of steps in the systems development life cycle (SDLC) is

   A. 4
   B. 5
   C. 6
   D. 10

10. Who is the person responsible for ensuring that the project is completed on time with the defined quality and specified budget constraints?

    A. Systems designer
    B. Project manager
    C. Systems owner
    D. Systems manager

11. Which of the following is the deliverable at the system implementation phase?

    A. A solution meeting the specific business needs
    B. Defined business problem
    C. Clear identification of business requirements
    D. A blueprint and sketch of the desired system

12. What type of mail requires proof of delivery?

    A. Express post
    B. External post
    C. Licensed post
    D. Registered post

13. Which of these is a good quality measure?

    A. Authority
    B. Correctness
    C. Precision
    D. All of the above

14. A group of related projects combine to form a _____.

    A. projects classification
    B. product
    C. department
    D. program

15. _____ analysis performs an assessment of internal and external environment.

    A. SWOT
    B. Comprehensive
    C. Organizational
    D. Strategic

16. A dummy activity is required when there is/are

    A. different ending events for more than one activity
    B. one ending event for more than one activity
    C. one starting event for two or more activities
    D. one starting and ending event for more than one activity in the network

17. Limitations of PERT and CPM include

    A. only a limited type of projects can be applied to these
    B. too much consideration is given to the critical path
    C. these are only to monitor the schedules
    D. it is difficult to interpret because of the graphical nature of the network

18. If there is a negative tracking signal against a forecasting, it means

    A. this forecast approach regularly underpredicts
    B. MAPE, too, will be negative
    C. this forecast approach regularly overpredicts
    D. MSE, too, will be negative

19. Quality management is the responsibility of

    A. team Leader
    B. team member
    C. quality assurance coordinator
    D. project manager

20. Purchasing insurance is considered what type of risk?

    A. Recognition
    B. Prevention
    C. Mitigation
    D. Transfer

21. Project costs may be monitored with respect to different categories with the help of

    A. standard accounting practices
    B. chart of accounts
    C. WBS
    D. UAS

22. What is the output of an administrative closure?

    A. Project documentation
    B. Project archives
    C. Risk analysis
    D. None of the above

23. A detailed project budget is created in the _____ process.

   A. establishment
   B. execution
   C. planning
   D. control

24. The person who can gain or lose something from the result of a project activity is the

   A. team member
   B. team leader
   C. supporter
   D. project manager

25. When a project manager apologizes for failing to deal with some issue, this is considered which of the following conflict resolutions?

   A. Forcing
   B. Withdrawal
   C. Compromising
   D. Collaborating

KEY (CORRECT ANSWERS)

1. C
2. C
3. C
4. C
5. A

6. C
7. B
8. B
9. C
10. B

11. A
12. D
13. D
14. D
15. A

16. D
17. B
18. C
19. D
20. D

21. B
22. B
23. C
24. C
25. B

EXAMINATION SECTION
TEST 1

DIRECTIONS: Each question or incomplete statement is followed by several suggested answers or completions. Select the one that BEST answers the question or completes the statement. *PRINT THE LETTER OF THE CORRECT ANSWER IN THE SPACE AT THE RIGHT.*

1. Management by exception (MBE) is

    A. designed to locate bottlenecks
    B. designed to pinpoint superior performance
    C. a form of index locating
    D. a form of variance reporting

2. In managerial terms, gap analysis is useful primarily in

    A. problem solving
    B. setting standards
    C. inventory control
    D. locating bottlenecks

3. ABC analysis involves

    A. problem solving
    B. indexing
    C. brainstorming
    D. inventory control

4. The Federal Discrimination in Employment Act as amended in 1978 prohibits job discrimination based on age for persons between the ages of

    A. 35 and 60   B. 40 and 65   C. 45 and 65   D. 40 and 70

5. Inspectors should be familiar with the contractor's CPM charts for a construction job primarily to determine if

    A. the job is on schedule
    B. the contractor is using the charts correctly
    C. material is on hand to keep the job on schedule
    D. there is a potential source of delay

6. The value engineering approach is frequently found in public works contracts. Value engineering is

    A. an effort to cut down or eliminate extra work payments
    B. a team approach to optimize the cost of the project
    C. to insure that material and equipment will perform as specified
    D. to insure that insurance costs on the project can be minimized

7. Historically, most costly claims have been either for

    A. unreasonable inspection requirements or unforeseen weather conditions
    B. unreasonable specification requirements or unreasonable completion time for the contract
    C. added costs due to inflation or unavailability of material
    D. delays or alleged charged conditions

8. A claim is a

   A. dispute that cannot be resolved
   B. dispute arising from ambiguity in the specifications
   C. dispute arising from the quality of the work
   D. recognition that the courts are the sole arbiters of a dispute

9. Disputes arising between a contractor and the owning agency are

   A. the result of inflexibility of either or both parties to the dispute
   B. mainly the result of shortcomings in the design
   C. the result of shortcomings in the specifications
   D. inevitable

Questions 10-13.

DIRECTIONS: Questions 10 through 13, inclusive, refers to the array of numbers listed below.

16, 7, 9, 5, 10, 8, 5, 1, 2

10. The mean of the numbers is

    A. 2 B. 5 C. 7 D. 8

11. The median of the numbers is

    A. 2 B. 5 C. 7 D. 8

12. The mode of the numbers is

    A. 2 B. 5 C. 7 D. 8

13. In statistical measurements, a subgroup that is representative of the entire group is a

    A. commutative group   B. sample
    C. central index   D. Abelian group

14. Productivity is the ratio of

    A. $\dfrac{\text{product costs}}{\text{labor costs}}$

    B. $\dfrac{\text{cost of final product}}{\text{cost of materials}}$

    C. $\dfrac{\text{outputs}}{\text{inputs}}$

    D. $\dfrac{\text{outputs cost}}{\text{time needed to product the output}}$

15. Downtime is the time a piece of equipment is

    A. idle waiting for other equipment to become available
    B. not being used for the purpose it was intended

C. being used inefficiently
D. unavailable for use

16. Index numbers

    A. relates to the cost of a product as material costs vary
    B. allows the user to find the variation from the norm
    C. are a way of comparing costs of different approaches to a problem
    D. a way of measuring and comparing changes over a period of time

17. The underlying idea behind Management by Objectives is to provide a mechanism for managers to

    A. coordinate personal and departmental plans with organizational goals
    B. motivate employees by having them participate in job decisions
    C. motivate employees by training them for the next higher position
    D. set objectives that are reasonable for the employees to attain, thus improving self-esteem among the employees

18. The ultimate objective of the project manager in planning and scheduling a project is to

    A. meet the completion dates of the project
    B. use the least amount of labor on the project
    C. use the least amount of material on the project
    D. prevent interference between the different trades

19. Scheduling with respect to the critical path method usually does not involve

    A. cost allocation
    B. starting and finishing time
    C. float for each activity
    D. project duration

20. When CPM is used on a construction project, updates are most commonly made

    A. weekly
    B. every two weeks
    C. monthly
    D. every two months

Questions 21-24.

DIRECTIONS: Questions 21 through 24 refer to the following network.

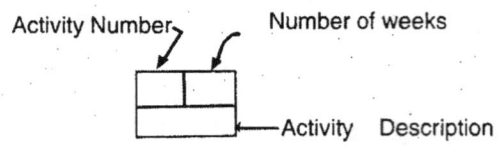

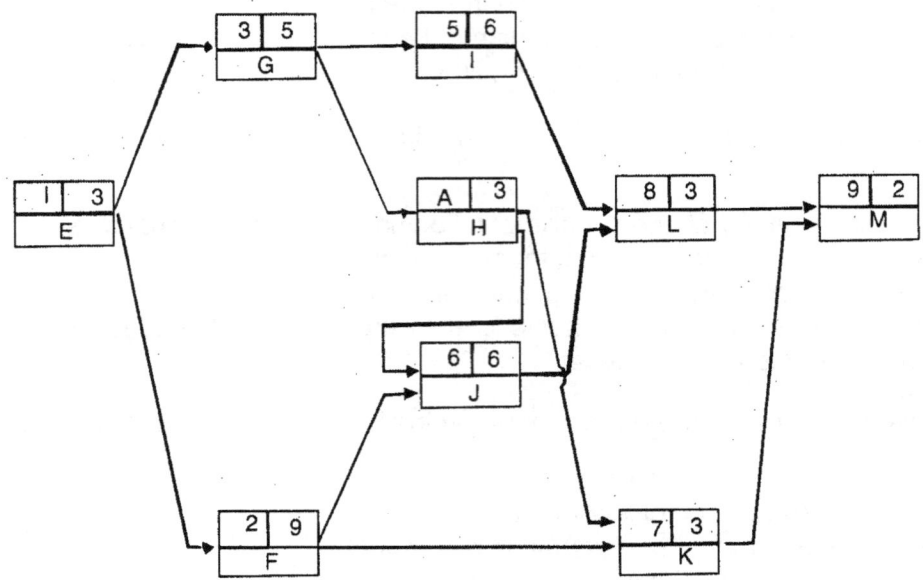

Activity Number	Activity Description	Duration in Weeks	Early Start	Early Finish	Late Start	Late Finish	Total Slack
1	E	3					
2	F	9					
3	G	5					
4	H	3					
5	I	6					
6	J	6					
7	K	3					
8	L	3					
9	M	2					

21. The critical path is

    A. E G H J L M   B. E G I L M
    C. E F J L M   D. E G H K M

21.____

22. The minimum time needed to complete the job is, in weeks,

    A. 19   B. 21   C. 22   D. 23

22.____

23. The slack time in J is, in weeks,

    A. 0   B. 1   C. 2   D. 3

23.____

24. The slack time in K is, in weeks,

    A. 4   B. 5   C. 6   D. 7

24.____

25. Of the following, the primary objective of CPM is to   25._____
   A. eliminate duplication of work
   B. overcome obstacles such as bad weather
   C. spot potential bottlenecks
   D. save on the cost of material

KEY (CORRECT ANSWERS)

1.	D	11.	C
2.	A	12.	B
3.	D	13.	B
4.	D	14.	C
5.	A	15.	D
6.	B	16.	D
7.	D	17.	A
8.	A	18.	A
9.	D	19.	A
10.	C	20.	C

21. C
22. D
23. A
24. C
25. C

TEST 2

DIRECTIONS: Each question or incomplete statement is followed by several suggested answers or completions. Select the one that BEST answers the question or completes the statement. *PRINT THE LETTER OF THE CORRECT ANSWER IN THE SPACE AT THE RIGHT.*

1. Gantt refers to

    A. bar charts
    B. milestone charts
    C. PERT networks
    D. Management by Objectives

2. PERT is an abbreviation for

    A. Progress Evaluation in Real Time
    B. Preliminary Evaluation of Running Time
    C. Program Evaluation Review Techniques
    D. Program Estimation and Repair Times

3. In project management terms, slack is equivalent to

    A. tare   B. off time   C. delay   D. float

4. The FIRST step in planning and programming a roadway pavement management system is to evaluate

    A. priorities for the work to be done
    B. the condition of your equipment
    C. the condition of the roads in the system
    D. the storage and maintenance facilities

5. Managers accomplish their work in an ever changing environment by integrating three time-tested approaches. The one of the following that is NOT a time-tested approach is

    A. scientific adaptation
    B. scientific management
    C. behavior management
    D. management sciences

6. The most effective managers manage for optimum results. This means that the manager is seeking to _____ a given situation.

    A. get the maximum results from
    B. get the most favorable results from
    C. get the most reasonable results from
    D. satisfy the conflicting interests in

7. If a manager believes that an employee is irresponsible, the employee, in subtle response to the manager's assessment, will in fact prove to be irresponsible. This is an example of a(n)

    A. conditioned reflex
    B. self-fulfilling prophesy
    C. Freudian response
    D. automatic reaction

8. Perhaps nothing distinguishes the younger generation from the older so much as the value placed on work. The older generation was generally raised to believe in the Protestant work ethic.
This ethic holds primarily that

A. people should try to get the highest salary possible
B. work should help people to advance
C. work should be well done if it is interesting
D. work is valuable in itself and the person who does it focuses on his work

9. The standard method currently in use in inspecting bituminous paving is to inspect each activity in detail as the paving work is being installed. In recent years some agencies use a different method of inspection known as a(n)

    A. as-built quality control method
    B. statistically controlled quality assurance method
    C. data based history of previous contracts of this type
    D. performance evaluation of the completed paving contract

9.____

10. Aggregates for use in bituminous pavements should be tested for grading,

    A. abrasion, soundness, and specific gravity
    B. type of rock, abrasion, and specific gravity
    C. abrasion, soundness, and deleterious material
    D. specific gravity, chemical composition of the aggregate, and deleterious material

10.____

11. Of the following, the one that is LEAST likely to be a test for asphalt is

    A. specific gravity   B. flashpoint
    C. viscosity   D. penetration

11.____

12. According to the AASHO, for bituminous pavements PSI is an abbreviation for _____ Index.

    A. Present Serviceability   B. Pavement Smoothness
    C. Pavement Serviceability   D. Present Smoothness

12.____

13. According to the AASHO, a bituminous pavement that is in extremely poor condition will have a PSI

    A. above 5.5   B. above 3.5
    C. below 3.5   D. below 1.5

13.____

14. The U.S. Federal Highway Administration defines asphalt maintenance as including work designed primarily for rejuvenation or protection of existing surfaces less than _____ inch minimum thickness.

    A. 1/4   B. 1/2   C. 3/4   D. 1

14.____

15. The maintenance phase of a highway management system includes the establishment of a program and schedule of work based largely on budget considerations, the actual operations of crack filling, patching, etc. and

    A. inspection of completed work
    B. planning of future operations
    C. upgrading existing pavements
    D. acquisition and processing of data

15.____

16. In a bituminous asphalt pavement, the progressive separation of aggregate particles in a pavement from the surface downward or from the edges inward is the definition of

   A. alligatoring
   B. raveling
   C. scaling
   D. disintegration

17. The bituminous pavement condition for the purpose of overlay design includes ride quality, structural capacity, skid resistance, and

   A. durability
   B. age of the pavement
   C. CBR value
   D. surface distress

18. An asphalt mix is being transferred from an asphalt truck to the hopper of the paving machine. Blue smoke rises from the material being emptied into the hopper of the paving machine.
   Your conclusion should be that

   A. this is normal and is to be expected
   B. the mix is overheated
   C. the mix is too cold
   D. the mix is being transferred too rapidly

19. Polished aggregate in an asphalt pavement are aggregate particles that have been rounded and polished smooth by traffic. This is a

   A. *good* condition as it allows a smooth ride
   B. *good* condition as it preserves tires
   C. *poor* condition as it promotes skidding
   D. *poor* condition as it tends to break the bond between the asphalt and the aggregate

20. A slippery asphalt surface requires a skid-resistant surfacing material. Of the following, the cover that would be most appropriate is a(n)

   A. asphalt tack coat
   B. fog seal
   C. layer of sand rolled into the asphalt surface
   D. asphalt emulsion slurry seal

21. The maximum size of aggregate in a hot mix asphalt concrete surfacing and bases allowed by the Federal Highway Administration Grading A is _____ inch(es).

   A. 3/4   B. 1   C. 1 1/4   D. 1 1/2

22. Wet sand weighs 132 pounds per cubic foot and contains 8% noisture. The dry weight of a cubic foot of sand is _____ pounds.

   A. 122.2   B. 122.0   C. 121.7   D. 121.4

23. A very light spray application of 551h emulsified asphalt diluted with water is used on existing pavement as a seal to riinimize raveling and to enrich the surface of a dried-out pavement is known as a(n)

   A. prime coat
   B. tack coat
   C. fog seal
   D. emulsion seal

24. 90 kilometers per hour is equivalent to _____ miles per hour.

   A. 49   B. 54   C. 59   D. 64

25. In a table of pavement distress manifestations is a column broadly titled *Density of Pavement Distress*.
   This is equivalent to _____ of the defects.

   A. average depth
   B. average area
   C. extent of occurrence
   D. seriousness

KEY (CORRECT ANSWERS)

1.	A	11.	A
2.	A	12.	A
3.	D	13.	D
4.	C	14.	C
5.	A	15.	D
6.	B	16.	B
7.	B	17.	D
8.	D	18.	B
9.	B	19.	C
10.	C	20.	D

21. D
22. A
23. C
24. B
25. C

EXAMINATION SECTION
TEST 1

DIRECTIONS: Each question or incomplete statement is followed by several suggested answers or completions. Select the one that BEST answers the question or completes the statement. *PRINT THE LETTER OF THE CORRECT ANSWER IN THE SPACE AT THE RIGHT.*

1. In many instances, managers deliberately set up procedures and routines that more than one department or more than one employee is required to complete and verify an entire operation or transaction.
   The MAIN reason for establishing such routines is *generally* to

   A. minimize the chances of gaps and deficiencies in feedback of information to management
   B. expand the individual employee's vision and concern for broader organizational objectives
   C. provide satisfaction of employees' social and egoistic needs through teamwork and horizontal communications
   D. facilitate internal control designed to prevent errors, whether intentional or accidental

   1.____

2. Committees—sometimes referred to as boards, commissions, or task forces—are widely used in government to investigate certain problems or to manage certain agencies.
   Of the following, the MOST serious limitation of the committee approach to management in government is that

   A. it reflects government's inability to delegate authority effectively to individual executives
   B. committee members do not usually have similar backgrounds, experience, and abilities
   C. it promotes horizontal communication at the expense of vertical communication
   D. the spreading out of responsibility to a committee often results in a willingness to settle for weak, compromise solutions

   2.____

3. Of the following, the BEST reason for replacing members of committees on a staggered or partial basis rather than replacing all members simultaneously is that this practice

   A. gives representatives of different interest groups a chance to contribute their ideas
   B. encourages continuity of policy since retained members are familiar with previous actions
   C. prevents interpersonal frictions from building up and hindering the work of the group
   D. improves the quality of the group's recommendations and decisions by stimulating development of new ideas

   3.____

4. Assume that in considering a variety of actions to take to solve a given problem, a manager decides to take no action at all.
   According to generally accepted management practice, such a decision would be

   4.____

A. *proper,* because under normal circumstances, it is better to make no decision
B. *improper,* because inaction would be rightly construed as shunning one's responsibilities
C. *proper,* since this would be a decision which might produce more positive results than the other alternatives
D. *improper,* since such a solution would delay corrective action and exacerbate the problem

5. Some writers in the field of management assume that when a newly promoted manager has been informed by his superior about the subordinates he is to direct and the extent of his authority, that is all that is necessary. However, thereafter, this new manager should realize that, for practical purposes, his authority will be effective ONLY when

   A. he accepts full responsibility for the actions of his subordinates
   B. his subordinates are motivated to carry out their assignments
   C. it derives from acceptable personal attributes rather than from his official position
   D. he exercises it in an authoritarian manner

6. A newly appointed manager is assigned to assist the head of a small developing agency handling innovative programs. Although this manager is a diligent worker, he does not delegate authority to middle- and lower-echelon supervisors. The MOST important reason why it would be desirable to change this attitude toward delegation is because otherwise

   A. he may have to assume more responsibility for the actions of his subordinates than is implied in the authority delegated to him
   B. his subordinates will tend to produce innovative solutions on their own
   C. the agency will become a decentralized type of organization in which he cannot maintain adequate controls
   D. he may not have time to perform other essential tasks

7. All types of organizations and all functions within them are to varying degrees affected today by the need to understand the application of computer systems to management practices.
The one of the following purposes for which such systems would be MOST useful is to

   A. lower the costs of problem-solving by utilizing data that is already in the agency's control system correlated with new data
   B. stabilize basic patterns of the organization into long-term structures and relationships
   C. give instant solutions to complex problems
   D. affect savings in labor costs for office tasks involving non-routine complex problems

8. Compared to individual decision-making, group decision-making is burdened with the DISADVANTAGE of

   A. making snap judgments
   B. pressure to examine all relevant elements of the problem
   C. greater motivation needed to implement the decision
   D. the need to clarify problems for the group participants

9. Assume that a manager in an agency, faced with a major administrative problem, has developed a number of alternative solutions to the problem.
Which of the following would be MOST effective in helping the manager make the best decision?

   A. *Experience,* because a manager can distill from the past the fundamental reasons for success or failure since the future generally duplicates the past
   B. *Experimentation,* because it is the method used in scientific inquiry and can be tried out economically in limited areas
   C. *Research analysis,* because it is generally less costly than most other methods and involves the interrelationships among the more critical factors that bear upon the goal sought
   D. *Value forecasting,* because it assigns numerical significance to the values of alternative tangible and intangible choices and indicates the degree of risk involved in each choice

10. Management information systems operate more effectively for managers than mere data tabulating systems because information systems

   A. eliminate the need for managers to tell information processors what is required
   B. are used primarily for staff rather than line functions
   C. are less expensive to operate than manual methods of data collection
   D. present and utilize data in a meaningful form

11. Project-type organizations are in widespread use today because they offer a number of advantages.
The MOST important purpose of the project organization is to

   A. secure a higher degree of coordination than could be obtained in a conventional line structure
   B. provide an orderly way of phasing projects in and out of organizations
   C. expedite routine administrative processes
   D. allow for rapid assessment of the status of any given project and its effect on agency productivity

12. A manager adjusts his plans for future activity by reviewing information about the performance of his subordinates. This is an application of the process of

   A. human factor impact   B. coordinated response
   C. feedback communication   D. reaction control

13. From the viewpoint of the manager in an agency, the one of the following which is the MOST constructive function of a status system or a rank system based on employee performance is that the system

   A. makes possible effective communication, thereby lessening social distances between organizational levels
   B. is helpful to employees of lesser ability because it provides them with an incentive to exceed their capacities
   C. encourages the employees to attain or exceed the goals set for them by the organization
   D. diminishes friction in assignment and work relation-ships of personnel

14. Some managers ask employees who have been newly hired by their agency and then assigned to their divisions or units such questions as: *What are your personal goals? What do you expect from your job? Why do you want to work for this organization?* For a manager to ask these questions is GENERALLY considered

    A. *inadvisable;* these questions should have been asked prior to hiring the employee
    B. *inadvisable;* the answers will arouse subjective prejudices in the manager before he sees what kind of work the employee can do
    C. *advisable;* this approach indicates to the employee that the manager is interested in him as an individual
    D. *advisable;* the manager can judge how much of a disparity exists between the employee's goals and the agency's goals

15. Assume that you have prepared a report to your superior recommending a reorganization of your staff to eliminate two levels of supervision. The total number of employees would remain the same, with the supervisors of the two eliminated levels taking on staff assignments.
    In your report, which one of the following should NOT be listed as an expected result of such a reorganization?

    A. Fewer breakdowns and distortions in communications to staff
    B. Greater need for training
    C. Broader opportunities for development of employee skills
    D. Fewer employee errors due to exercise of closer supervision and control

16. *Administration* has often been criticized as being unproductive in the sense that it seems far removed from the end products of an organization.
    According to modern management thought, this criticism, for the most part, is

    A. *invalid,* because administrators make it possible for subordinates to produce goods or services by directing coordinating, and controlling their activities
    B. *valid,* because most subordinates usually do the work required to produce goods and services with only general direction from their immediate superiors
    C. *invalid,* because administrators must see to all of the details associated with the production of services
    D. *valid,* because administrators generally work behind the scenes and are mainly concerned with long-range planning

17. A manager must be able to evaluate the relative importance of his decisions and establish priorities for carrying them out.
    Which one of the following factors bearing on the relative importance of making a decision would indicate to a manager that he can delegate that decision to a subordinate or give it low priority? The

    A. decision concerns a matter on which strict confiden-tiality must be maintained
    B. community impact of the decision is great
    C. decision can be easily changed
    D. decision commits the agency to a heavy expenditure of funds

18. Suppose that you are responsible for reviewing and submitting to your superior the monthly reports from ten field auditors. Despite your repeated warnings to these auditors, most of them hand in their reports close to or after the deadline dates, so that you have no time to return them for revision and find yourself working overtime to make the necessary corrections yourself.
The deadline dates for the auditors' reports and your report cannot be changed.
Of the following, the MOST probable cause for this con-tinuing situation is that

    A. these auditors need retraining in the writing of this type of report
    B. possible disciplinary action as a result of the delay by the auditors has not been impressed upon them
    C. the auditors have had an opportunity to provide you with feedback to explain the reasons for the delays
    D. you, as the manager, have not used disciplinary measures of sufficient severity to change their behavior

19. Assume that an agency desiring to try out a *management-by-objectives* program has set down the guidelines listed below to implement this activity.
Which one of these guidelines is MOST likely to present obstacles to the success of this type of program?

    A. Specific work objectives should be determined by top management for employees at all levels.
    B. Objectives should be specific, attainable, and preferably measurable as to units, costs, ratios, time, etc.
    C. Standards of performance should be either qualitative or quantitative, preferably quantitative.
    D. There should be recognition and rewards for success-ful achievement of objectives.

20. Of the following, the MOST meaningful way to express productivity where employees work a standard number of hours each day is in terms of the relationship between man-

    A. hours expended and number of work-units needed to produce the final product
    B. days expended and goods and services produced
    C. days and energy expended
    D. days expended and number of workers

21. Agencies often develop productivity indices for many of their activities.
Of the following, the MOST important use for such indices is *generally* to

    A. measure the agency's output against its own past performance
    B. improve quality standards while letting productivity remain unchanged
    C. compare outputs of the agency with outputs in private industry
    D. determine manpower requirements

22. The MOST outstanding characteristic of staff authority, such as that of a public relations officer in an agency, as compared with line authority, is *generally* accepted to be

    A. reliance upon personal attributes
    B. direct relationship to the primary objectives of the organization
    C. absence of the right to direct or command
    D. responsibility for attention to technical details

23. In the traditional organization structure, there are often more barriers to upward communication than to downward communication.
    From the viewpoint of a manager whose goal is to overcome obstacles to communication, this situation should be

    A. *accepted;* the downward system is the more important since it is highly directive, giving necessary orders, instructions, and procedures
    B. *changed;* the upward system should receive more emphasis than the downward system, which represents stifling bureaucratic authority
    C. *accepted;* it is generally conceded that upward systems supply enough feedback for control purposes necessary to the organization's survival
    D. *changed;* research has generally verified the need for an increase in upward communications to supply more information about employees' ideas, attitudes, and performance

24. A principal difficulty in productivity measurement for local government services is in defining and measuring output, a problem familiar to managers. A measurement that merely looks good, but which may be against the public interest, is another serious problem. Managers should avoid encouraging employees to take actions that lead to such measurements.
    In accordance with the foregoing statement, it would be MOST desirable for a manager to develop a productivity measure that

    A. correlates the actual productivity measure with impact on benefit to the citizenry
    B. does not allow for a mandated annual increase in productivity
    C. firmly fixes priorities for resource allocations
    D. uses numerical output, by itself, in productivity incentive plans

25. For a manager, the MOST significant finding of the Hawthorne studies and experiments is that an employee's productivity is affected MOST favorably when the

    A. importance of tasks is emphasized and there is a logical arrangement of work functions
    B. physical surroundings and work conditions are improved
    C. organization has a good public relations program
    D. employee is given recognition and allowed to participate in decision-making

KEY (CORRECT ANSWERS)

1. D
2. D
3. B
4. C
5. B

6. D
7. A
8. D
9. C
10. D

11. A
12. C
13. C
14. A
15. D

16. A
17. C
18. D
19. A
20. B

21. A
22. C
23. D
24. A
25. D

TEST 2

DIRECTIONS: Each question or incomplete statement is followed by several suggested answers or completions. Select the one that BEST answers the question or completes the statement. *PRINT THE LETTER OF THE CORRECT ANSWER IN THE SPACE AT THE RIGHT.*

1. Which one of the following is generally accepted by managers as the MOST difficult aspect of a training program in staff supervision?

    A. Determining training needs of the staff
    B. Evaluating the effectiveness of the courses
    C. Locating capable instructors to teach the courses
    D. Finding adequate space and scheduling acceptable times for all participants

2. Assume that, as a manager, you have decided to start a job enrichment program with the purpose of making jobs more varied and interesting in an effort to increase the motivation of a certain group of workers in your division. Which one of the following should generally NOT be part of this program?

    A. Increasing the accountability of these individuals for their own work
    B. Granting additional authority or job freedom to these employees in their job activities
    C. Mandating increased monthly production goals for this group of employees
    D. Giving each of these employees a complete unit of work

3. Both employer and employee have an important stake in effective preparation for retirement.
   According to modern management thinking, the one of the following which is probably the MOST important aspect of a sound pre-retirement program is to

    A. make assignments that utilize the employee's abilities fully
    B. reassign the employee to a less demanding position in the organization for the last year or two he is on the job
    C. provide the employee with financial data and other facts that would be pertinent to his retirement planning
    D. encourage the employee to develop interests and hobbies which are connected with the job

4. The civil service system generally emphasizes a policy of *promotion-from-within.* Employees in the direct line of promotion in a given occupational group are eligible for promotion to the next higher title in that occupational group.
   Which one of the following is LEAST likely to occur as a result of this policy and practice?

    A. Training time will be saved since employees in higher-level positions are already familiar with many agency rules, regulations, and procedures.
    B. The recruitment section will be able to show prospective employees that there are distinct promotional opportunities.
    C. Employees will be provided with a clear-cut picture as to their possible career ladder.
    D. Employees will be encouraged to seek broad-based training and education to enhance their promotability.

5. From a management point of view, the MAIN drawback of seniority as opposed to merit as a basis for granting pay increases to workers is that a pay increase system based on seniority

   A. is favored by unions
   B. upsets organizational status relationships
   C. may encourage mediocre performance by employees
   D. is more difficult to administer than a merit plan

6. One of the actions that is often taken against employees in the non-uniformed forces who are accused of misconduct on the job is suspension without pay.
   The MOST justifiable reason for taking such action is to

   A. ease an employee out of the agency
   B. enable an investigation to be conducted into the circumstances of the offense where doubt exists about the guilt of the employee
   C. improve the performance of the employee when he returns to the job
   D. punish the employee by imposing a hardship on him

7. A manager has had difficulty in getting good clerical employees to staff a filing section under his supervision. To add to his problems, one of his most competent senior clerks requests a transfer to the accounting division so that he can utilize his new accounting skill, which he is acquiring by going to college at night. The manager attempts to keep the senior clerk in his filing section by calling the director of personnel and getting him to promise not to authorize any transfer. GENERALLY, this manager's action is

   A. *desirable;* he should not help his staff to develop themselves if it means losing good people
   B. *undesirable;* he should recommend that the senior clerk get a raise in the hope of preventing him from transferring to another section
   C. *desirable;* it shows that the manager is concerned about the senior clerk's future performance
   D. *undesirable;* it is good policy to transfer employees to the type of work they are interested in and for which they are acquiring training

8. One of your subordinates, a unit supervisor, comes to you, the division chief, because he feels that he is working out of title, and he suggests that his competitive class position should be reclassified to a higher title.
   Which one of the following statements that the subordinate has made is generally LEAST likely to be a valid support for his suggestion?

   A. The work he is doing conforms to the general statement of duties and responsibilities as described in the class specification for the next higher title in his occupational group.
   B. Most of the typical tasks he performs are listed in the class specification for a title with a higher salary range and are not listed for his current title.
   C. His education and experience qualifications far exceed the minimum requirements for the position he holds.
   D. His duties and responsibilities have changed recently and are now similar to those of his supervisor.

9. Assume that a class specification for a competitive title used exclusively by your agency is outdated, and that no examination for the title has been given since the specification was issued.
Of the following, the MOST appropriate action for your agency to take is to

   A. make the necessary changes and submit the revised class specification to the city civil service commission
   B. write the personnel director to recommend that the class specification be updated, giving the reasons and suggested revisions
   C. prepare a revised class specification and submit it to the office of management and budget for their approval
   D. secure approval of the state civil service commission to update the class specification, and then submit the revised specification to the city civil service commission

10. Assume that an appropriate eligible list has been established and certified to your agency for a title in which a large number of provisionals are serving in your agency. In order to obtain permission from the personnel director to retain some of them beyond the usual time limit set by rules (two months) following certification of the list, which one of the following conditions MUST apply?

   A. The positions are sensitive and require investigation of eligibles prior to appointment.
   B. Replacement of all provisionals within two months would impair essential public service.
   C. Employees are required to work rotating shifts, including nights and weekends.
   D. The duties of the positions require unusual physical effort and endurance.

11. Under the federally-funded Comprehensive Employment and Training Act (CETA), the hiring by the city of non-civil servants for CETA jobs is PROHIBITED when the

   A. applicants are unemployed because of seasonal lay-offs in private industry
   B. applicants do not meet U.S. citizenship and city residence requirements
   C. jobs have minimum requirements of specialized professional or technical training and experience
   D. jobs are comparable to those performed by laid-off civil servants

12. Assume you are in charge of the duplicating service in your agency. Since employees assigned to this operation lack a sense of accomplishment because the work is highly specialized and repetitive, your superior proposes to enlarge the jobs of these workers and asks you about your reaction to this strategy.
The MOST appropriate response for you to make is that job enlargement would be

   A. *undesirable*, PRIMARILY because it would increase production costs
   B. *undesirable*, PRIMARILY because it would diminish the quality of the output
   C. *desirable*, PRIMARILY because it might make it possible to add an entire level of management to the organizational structure of your agency
   D. *desirable*, PRIMARILY because it might make it possible to decrease the amount of supervision the workers will require

13. According to civil service law, layoff or demotion must be made in inverse order of seniority among employees permanently serving in the same title and layoff unit. Which one of the following is now the CORRECT formula for computing seniority?
Total continuous service in the

A. competitive class *only*
B. competitive, non-competitive, or labor class
C. classified or unclassified services
D. competitive, non-competitive, exempt, and labor classes

14. Under which of the following conditions would an appointing officer be permitted to consider the sex of a candidate in making an employment decision?
When

    A. the duties of the position require considerable physical effort or strength
    B. the duties of the position are considered inherently dangerous
    C. separate toilet facilities and dressing rooms for the sexes are unavailable and/or cannot be provided in any event
    D. the public has indicated a preference to be served by persons of a specified sex

15. Assume that an accountant under your supervision signs out to the field to make an agency audit. It is later discovered that, although he had reported himself at work until 5 P.M. that day, he had actually left for home at 3:30 P.M. Although this accountant has worked for the city for ten years and has had an excellent performance record, he is demoted to a lower title in punishment for this breach of duty.
According to generally accepted thinking on personnel management, the disciplinary action taken in this case should be considered

    A. *appropriate;* a lesser penalty might encourage repetition of the offense
    B. *inappropriate;* the correct penalty for such a breach of duty should be dismissal
    C. *appropriate;* the accountant's abilities may be utilized better in the new assignment
    D. *inappropriate;* the impact of a continuing stigma and loss of salary is not commensurate with the offense committed

16. Line managers often request more funds for their units than are actually required to attain their current objectives.
Which one of the following is the MOST important reason for such inflated budget requests?
The

    A. expectation that budget examiners will exercise their prerogative of budget cutting
    B. line manager's interest in improving the performance of his unit is thereby indicated to top management
    C. expectation that such requests will make it easier to obtain additional funds in future years
    D. opinion that it makes sense to obtain additional funds and decide later how to use them

17. Integrating budgeting with program planning and evaluation in a city agency is GENERALLY considered to be

    A. *undesirable;* budgeting must focus on the fiscal year at hand, whereas planning must concern itself with developments over a period of years
    B. *desirable;* budgeting facilitates the choice-making process by evaluating the financial implications of agency programs and forcing cost comparisons among them
    C. *undesirable;* accountants and statisticians with the required budgetary skills have little familiarity with the substantive programs that the agency is conducting
    D. *desirable;* such a partnership increases the budgetary skills of planners, thus promoting more effective use of public resources

18. As an aspect of the managerial function, a budget is described BEST as a

    A. set of qualitative management controls over productivity
    B. tool based on historical accounting reports
    C. type of management plan expressed in quantitative terms
    D. precise estimate of future quantitative and qualitative contingencies

19. Which one of the following is *generally* accepted as the MAJOR immediate advantage of installing a system of program budgeting?
    It

    A. encourages managers to relate their decisions to the agency's long-range goals
    B. is a replacement for the financial or fiscal budget
    C. decreases the need for managers to make trade-offs in the decision-making process
    D. helps to adjust budget figures to provide for unexpected developments

20. Of the following, the BEST means for assuring necessary responsiveness of a budgetary program to changing conditions is by

    A. overestimating budgetary expenditures by 15% and assigning the excess to unforeseen problem areas
    B. underestimating budgetary expenditures by at least 20% and setting aside a reserve account in the same amount
    C. reviewing and revising the budget at regular intervals so that it retains its character as a current document
    D. establishing *budget by exception* policies for each division in the agency

21. According to expert thought in the area of budgeting, participation in the preparation of a government agency's budget should GENERALLY involve

    A. only top management
    B. only lower levels of management
    C. all levels of the organization
    D. only a central budget office or bureau

22. Of the following, the MOST useful guide to analysis of budget estimates for the coming fiscal year is a com-parison with

    A. appropriations as amended for the current fiscal year
    B. manpower requirements for the previous two years
    C. initial appropriations for the current fiscal year
    D. budget estimates for the preceding five years

23. A manager assigned to analyze the costs and benefits associated with a program which the agency head proposes to undertake may encounter certain factors which cannot be measured in dollar terms.
    In such a case, the manager should GENERALLY

    A. ignore the factors which cannot be quantified
    B. evaluate the factors in accordance with their degree of importance to the overall agency goals

C. give the factors weight equal to the weight given to measurable costs and benefits
D. assume that non-measurable costs and benefits will balance out against one another

24. If city employees believe that they are receiving adverse treatment in terms of training and disciplinary actions because of their national origin, they may file charges of discrimination with the Federal government's

   A. Human Rights Commission
   B. Public Employee Relations Board
   C. Equal Employment Opportunity Commission
   D. United States Department of Commerce

25. Under existing employment statutes, the city is obligated, as an employer, to take *affirmative action* in certain instances.
    This requirement has been imposed to ensure that

   A. employees who are members of minority groups, or women, be given special opportunities for training and promotion even though they are not available to other employees
   B. employees or applicants for employment are treated without regard to race, color, religion, sex, or national origin
   C. proof exists to show that the city has acted with good intentions in any case where it has disregarded this requirement
   D. men and women are treated alike except where State law provides special hour or working conditions for women

KEY (CORRECT ANSWERS)

1. B
2. C
3. C
4. D
5. C

6. B
7. D
8. C
9. B
10. B

11. D
12. D
13. D
14. C
15. D

16. A
17. B
18. C
19. A
20. C

21. C
22. A
23. B
24. C
25. B

EXAMINATION SECTION
TEST 1

DIRECTIONS: Each question or incomplete statement is followed by several suggested answers or completions. Select the one that BEST answers the question or completes the statement. *PRINT THE LETTER OF THE CORRECT ANSWER IN THE SPACE AT THE RIGHT.*

1. In organizational theory, the optimum span of control, that is, the number of subordinates who can be effectively supervised by one man above the level of the first line supervisor, is GENERALLY set at between

    A. 3 and 6   B. 6 and 12   C. 12 and 18   D. 18 and 24

2. Which of the following is LEAST desirable as a basic guide to normal conventional office layout?

    A. Arrange desks so that work flows in a normal fashion.
    B. Place files nearest to the persons who will use them.
    C. Utilize a number of small areas to provide privacy.
    D. Utilize one single large area.

3. *A set of objects together with relationships between the objects and between their attributes* is the definition of

    A. a perceptual whole and its subcomponents
    B. a system in the terms of specific systems theory
    C. an organism
    D. forms control

4. A technique of time study in which each employee maintains a record of his own time is GENERALLY known as _____ study.

    A. estimated time   B. observed time
    C. time log   D. wristwatch

5. An employee has approached a supervisor with a request for a change involving his personal status or with a suggestion for making an improvement in the work. The supervisor knows that the suggestion cannot be granted.
   Of the following, the BEST procedure would be for the supervisor to

    A. refer the matter to the personnel department
    B. refer the matter to his superior for action
    C. reject the proposal, explaining the defects or objections which cannot be overcome
    D. shelve the idea so that the employee will realize it cannot be acted upon

6. There are, in general, a number of common methods of drawing samples for statistical work.
   The method in which a regularly ordered interval is maintained between the items chosen is BEST termed _____ sampling.

    A. random   B. stratified or selective
    C. systematic   D. work

7. The multi-column process chart can be put to all of the following general uses EXCEPT to

   A. improve office layout
   B. improve procedures
   C. standardize procedures
   D. train personnel

8. If one wished to show the percentage of change over a period of time, the MOST appropriate type of graph or chart GENERALLY would be the _____ chart.

   A. bar
   B. line or curve
   C. logarithmic or semi-logarithmic
   D. pie

9. A chart designed for the explicit purpose of portraying graphically information relating to the degree of responsibility of key individuals for the performance of various functions is BEST described as a(n) _____ chart.

   A. linear responsibility
   B. work distribution
   C. work process
   D. staff

10. The technique of work measurement LEAST useful for setting up a program of office incentive pay GENERALLY would be

    A. log sheets
    B. stopwatch time study
    C. wristwatch time study
    D. work sampling

11. There are a number of steps to be taken in making a work sampling study in order to set production standards. Three of the steps listed below are peculiar only to work sampling, in contrast with other work measurement techniques. The one EXCEPTION is:

    A. Define the breakdown of work into the proper elements of work and no-work or delay to be observed
    B. Determine the required number of observations needed for the specified degree of reliability
    C. Establish the observation intervals
    D. Make a preliminary estimate of work and no-work or delay element percentages for step A

12. A number of standardized flow process chart symbols have been generally accepted. The symbol $\bar{v}$ GENERALLY indicates a(n)

    A. delay
    B. storage or file
    C. inspection
    D. operation

13. A number of standardized flow process chart symbols have been generally accepted. The symbol ▭ GENERALLY indicates a(n)

    A. delay
    B. storage or file
    C. inspection
    D. operation

14. The type of work for which short interval scheduling generally would be LEAST applicable would be the work of a group of

    A. calculating clerks
    B. order clerks
    C. technically-oriented clerks
    D. typists

15. In writing a business report, the BEST expression to use, in general, of those listed below would NORMALLY be:

    A. Because
    B. Inasmuch as
    C. In view of the fact that
    D. With reference to

16. Of the following, the MAJOR advantage of a random access data processing system, as compared with a sequential-type system, is its

    A. ability to use more than one input system
    B. demand for more sophisticated systems and programming
    C. greater storage capacity and access speed
    D. potential for processing data on a *first-come, first-served* basis

17. A good rule to remember with regard to decision making is that decisions should be made

    A. at the highest level competent to make such a decision
    B. at the lowest level competent to make such a decision
    C. by the person responsible for carrying out the decision
    D. by the person responsible for the work of the unit

18. Which of the following potential systems would LEAST likely be improved by being on-line? A(n) ____ system.

    A. budgeting control
    B. welfare eligibility
    C. employee payroll
    D. inventory control

19. A management information and control system essentially should be designed to provide management personnel with up-to-date information which will enable them to improve control over their operations.
    In designing such a system, the FIRST step to determine is:

    A. What information is needed to effectively control operations?
    B. What information is presently available?
    C. What organization changes are necessary to implement the system?
    D. Who is presently processing the information that might be used?

20. In designing control reports, which of the following guidelines is of MOST importance?

    A. Financial information should always be carried to the nearest penny.
    B. The report should be a simple and concise statement of only the pertinent facts
    C. The report should indicate the source of original data and how the computations were made.
    D. The report should have the broadest possible distribution at all levels of management.

21. A situation which enables a number of users at remote locations to have access to a SINGLE computer is called

    A. multiprocessing
    B. multiprogramming
    C. process overlap
    D. time sharing

22. The computer device which would offer the GREATEST speed in reading input is the

    A. CRT display
    B. magnetic tape
    C. optical scanner
    D. paper tape

23. Which of the following steps is LEAST desirable in designing an electronic data processing system?

    A. Design the EDP system first, then relate it to current operations.
    B. Develop a corollary chart for the corresponding flow of information
    C. Develop a flow chart for the functions affected by the system
    D. Obtain from available EDP equipment that which best fits current operations

24. Electronic data processing equipment can produce more information faster than can be generated by any other means. Because this is true, one wonders whether our ability to generate information has not far outstripped our ability to assimilate it.
    In view of this, a PERSISTENT danger management faces is in

    A. determining the budget for management information systems
    B. determining what information is of real worth
    C. finding enough computer personnel
    D. keeping their computers fully occupied

25. The one of the following that is an ADVANTAGE of a visual display terminal over the typewriter-type terminal employed in an on-line system is:

    A. Information retrieval is somewhat faster
    B. Operators can be trained more easily
    C. There is no advantage
    D. They are less expensive to operate

KEY (CORRECT ANSWERS)

1. A
2. C
3. A
4. C
5. C

6. C
7. A
8. C
9. A
10. A

11. A
12. B
13. C
14. C
15. A

16. D
17. B
18. C
19. A
20. B

21. D
22. A
23. A
24. B
25. A

TEST 2

DIRECTIONS: Each question or incomplete statement is followed by several suggested answers or completions. Select the one that BEST answers the question or completes the statement. *PRINT THE LETTER OF THE CORRECT ANSWER IN THE SPACE AT THE RIGHT.*

1. In analyzing data for the acquisition of new equipment, an analyst gathers the facts, analyzes them, and develops new procedures which will be required when the new equipment arrives.
In analyzing the factors involved, which one of the following is normally LEAST important in the evaluation of new equipment?

   A. Cost factors
   B. Layout and installation factors
   C. Production planning
   D. Operational experience of manufacturers of allied equipment

   1.____

2. If an analyst is required to recommend the selection of a machine for an office operation, he can BEST judge the expected output of a particular machine by pursuing which of the following courses of action?
Obtain

   A. an actual test run of the machine in his office
   B. data from the manufacturer of the machine
   C. information on the percentage of working time the machine will be used
   D. the experience of actual users of similar machines elsewhere

   2.____

3. Of the following, the BEST definition of records management is

   A. storage of all types of records at minimum expense
   B. planned control of all types of records
   C. storage of records for maximum accessibility
   D. systematic filing of all types of records

   3.____

4. The one of the following which is NOT a primary objective of a records retention and disposal system is to

   A. assure appropriate preservation of records having permanent value
   B. dispose of records not warranting further preservation
   C. establish retention standards for archives
   D. provide an opportunity to use miniaturization

   4.____

5. Of the following functions of management, the one which should NORMALLY precede the others is

   A. coordinating
   B. directing
   C. organizing
   D. planning

   5.____

6. One of the more famous studies of organizations is called the Hawthorne study. This work was one of the first to point out the importance of

   A. employee's benefit and retirement programs
   B. informal organization among employees
   C. job engineering
   D. styles of position classification

7. In organization theory, the type of position in which an individual is appointed to give technical aid to management on a particular problem area is generally BEST termed a(n)

   A. administrative assistant
   B. assistant to
   C. staff assistant
   D. staff specialist

8. In organizing, doing what *works* in the particular situation, with due regard to both short and long range objectives, is BEST termed

   A. ambivalence
   B. authoritarianism
   C. decentralization
   D. pragmatism

9. If an effort were made to reduce the number of private offices in a new layout, the LEAST effective substitute in offering privacy would be the use of

   A. an open area with lower movable partitions or railings separating each individual.
   B. conference rooms
   C. larger desks
   D. modular desk units

10. The term *administrative substation* NORMALLY refers to

    A. a work station handling a number of office services for an office organization
    B. a work station where middle level supervisors are located
    C. an office for handling management trainees
    D. the functions allocated to particular levels of administrative managers

11. An operations research technique which would be applied to determine the optimum number of window clerks or interviewers to have in an agency serving the public would MOST likely be the use of

    A. line of balance
    B. queuing theory
    C. simulation
    D. work sampling

12. A type of file which permits the operator to remain seated while the file can be moved backward and forward as required is BEST termed a _____ file.

    A. lateral
    B. movable
    C. reciprocating
    D. rotary

13. The technique of work measurement in which the analyst observes the work at random times of the day is BEST termed

    A. indirect observation
    B. logging
    C. ratio delay
    D. wristwatch

14. Examples of predetermined time systems generally should include all of the following EXCEPT 14._____

    A. Master Clerical Data
    B. Methods Time Measurement
    C. Short Interval Data
    D. Work Factor

15. A technique by which the supervisor or an assistant distributes a predetermined batch of work to the employees at periodic intervals of the day is generally BEST known as 15._____

    A. backlog control scheduling
    B. production control scheduling
    C. short interval scheduling
    D. workload balancing

16. E. Wright Bakke defined his *fusion process* as: The 16._____

    A. work environment to some degree remakes the organization and the organization to some degree remakes the work environment
    B. fusing of the interests of both management and labor unions
    C. community of interest between first line supervisors and top management
    D. organization to some degree remakes the individual and the individual to some degree remakes the organization

17. The title of a recent best-selling book by Robert Townsend is: 17._____

    A. MANAGEMENT ANALYSIS: WAVE OF THE FUTURE
    B. MANAGEMENT FOR RESULTS
    C. THE HUMAN SIDE OF ENTERPRISE
    D. UP THE ORGANIZATION

18. In planning office space for a newly established bureau, it would usually be LEAST desirable to 18._____

    A. concentrate, rather than disperse, the chief sources of office noises
    B. design an office environment with about the same brightness as the office desk
    C. designate as reception rooms, washrooms and other service areas those areas that will receive lesser amounts of illumination than those areas in which private office work will be performed
    D. eliminate natural light in cases where it is not the major light source

19. A private office should be used when its use is dictated by facts and unbiased judgment. It should never be provided simply because requests and sometimes pressure have been brought to bear.
    Of the following reasons used to justify use of a private office, the one that requires the MOST care in determining whether a private office is actually warranted is 19._____

    A. an office has always been provided for a particular job
    B. prestige considerations
    C. the confidential nature of the work
    D. the work involves high concentration

20. Theoretically, an ideal organization structure can be set up for each enterprise. In actual practice, the ideal organization structure is seldom, if ever, obtained.
Of the following, the one that normally is of LEAST influence in determining the organization structure is the

    A. existence of agreements and favors among members of the organization
    B. funds available
    C. opinions and beliefs of top executives
    D. tendency of management to discard established forms in favor of new forms

21. An IMPORTANT aspect to keep in mind during the decision-making process is that

    A. all possible alternatives for attaining goals should be sought out and considered
    B. considering various alternatives only leads to confusion
    C. once a decision has been made, it cannot be retracted
    D. there is only one correct method to reach any goal

22. Implementation of accountability requires

    A. a leader who will not hesitate to take punitive action
    B. an established system of communication from the bottom to the top
    C. explicit directives from leaders
    D. too much expense to justify it

23. Of the following, the MAJOR difference between systems and procedures analysis and work simplification is:

    A. The former complicates organizational routine and the latter simplifies it
    B. The former is objective and the latter is subjective
    C. The former generally utilizes expert advice and the latter is a *do-it-yourself* improvement by supervisors and workers
    D. There is no difference other than in name

24. Systems development is concerned with providing

    A. a specific set of work procedures
    B. an overall framework to describe general relationships
    C. definitions of particular organizational functions
    D. organizational symbolism

25. Organizational systems and procedures should be

    A. developed as problems arise as no design can anticipate adequately the requirements of an organization
    B. developed jointly by experts in systems and procedures and the people who are responsible for implementing them
    C. developed solely by experts in systems and procedures
    D. eliminated whenever possible to save unnecessary expense

KEY (CORRECT ANSWERS)

1.	D	11.	B
2.	A	12.	C
3.	B	13.	C
4.	D	14.	C
5.	D	15.	C
6.	B	16.	D
7.	D	17.	D
8.	D	18.	D
9.	C	19.	A
10.	A	20.	D

21. A
22. B
23. C
24. B
25. B

TEST 3

DIRECTIONS: Each question or incomplete statement is followed by several suggested answers or completions. Select the one that BEST answers the question or completes the statement. *PRINT THE LETTER OF THE CORRECT ANSWER IN THE SPACE AT THE RIGHT.*

1. The CHIEF danger of a decentralized control system is that

   A. excessive reports and communications will be generated
   B. problem areas may not be detected readily
   C. the expense will become prohibitive
   D. this will result in too many *chiefs*

2. Of the following, management guides and controls clerical work PRINCIPALLY through

   A. close supervision and constant checking of personnel
   B. spot checking of clerical procedures
   C. strong sanctions for clerical supervisors
   D. the use of printed forms

3. Which of the following is MOST important before conducting fact-finding interviews?

   A. Becoming acquainted with all personnel to be interviewed
   B. Explaining the techniques you plan to use
   C. Explaining to the operating officials the purpose and scope of the study
   D. Orientation of the physical layout

4. Of the following, the one that is NOT essential in carrying out a comprehensive work improvement program is

   A. standards of performance
   B. supervisory training
   C. work count/task list
   D. work distribution chart

5. Which of the following control techniques is MOST useful on large complex systems projects?

   A. A general work plan
   B. Gantt chart
   C. Monthly progress report
   D. PERT chart

6. The action which is MOST effective in gaining acceptance of a study by the agency which is being studied is

   A. a directive from the agency head to install a study based on recommendations included in a report
   B. a lecture-type presentation following approval of the procedures
   C. a written procedure in narrative form covering the proposed system with visual presentations and discussions
   D. procedural charts showing the *before* situation, forms, steps, etc. to the employees affected

7. Which of the following is NOT an advantage in the use of oral instructions as compared with written instructions? Oral instruction(s)

   A. can easily be changed
   B. is superior in transmitting complex directives
   C. facilitate exchange of information between a superior and his subordinate
   D. with discussions make it easier to ascertain understanding

8. Which organization principle is MOST closely related to procedural analysis and improvement?

   A. Duplication, overlapping, and conflict should be eliminated.
   B. Managerial authority should be clearly defined.
   C. The objectives of the organization should be clearly defined.
   D. Top management should be freed of burdensome detail.

9. Which one of the following is the MAJOR objective of operational audits?

   A. Detecting fraud
   B. Determining organization problems
   C. Determining the number of personnel needed
   D. Recommending opportunities for improving operating and management practices

10. Of the following, the formalization of organization structure is BEST achieved by

    A. a narrative description of the plan of organization
    B. functional charts
    C. job descriptions together with organization charts
    D. multi-flow charts

11. Budget planning is MOST useful when it achieves

    A. cost control
    B. forecast of receipts
    C. performance review
    D. personnel reduction

12. The UNDERLYING principle of sound administration is to

    A. base administration on investigation of facts
    B. have plenty of resources available
    C. hire a strong administrator
    D. establish a broad policy

13. Although questionnaires are not the best survey tool the management analyst has to use, there are times when a good questionnaire can expedite the *fact-finding* phase of a management survey.
Which of the following should be AVOIDED in the design and distribution of the questionnaire?

    A. Questions should be framed so that answers can be classified and tabulated for analysis.
    B. Those receiving the questionnaire must be knowledgeable enough to accurately provide the information desired.
    C. The questionnaire should enable the respondent to answer in a narrative manner.
    D. The questionnaire should require a minimum amount of writing.

13._____

14. Of the following, the formula which is used to calculate the arithmetic mean from data grouped in a frequency distribution is:

    A. $M = \dfrac{N}{\Sigma f \chi}$ B. $M = N(\Sigma f \chi)$ C. $M = \dfrac{\Sigma f \chi}{N}$ D. $M = \dfrac{\Sigma \chi}{fN}$

14._____

15. Arranging large groups of numbers in frequency distributions

    A. gives a more composite picture of the total group than a random listing
    B. is misleading in most cases
    C. is unnecessary in most instances
    D. presents the data in a form whereby further manipulation of the group is eliminated

15._____

16. After a budget has been developed, it serves to

    A. assist the accounting department in posting expenditures
    B. measure the effectiveness of department managers
    C. provide a yardstick against which actual costs are measured
    D. provide the operating department with total expenditures to date

16._____

17. Of the following, which formula is used to determine staffing requirements?

    A. $\dfrac{\text{Hours per man-Day}}{\text{Volume} \times \text{standard}} = \text{Employees Needed}$

    B. $\dfrac{\text{Hours per man-Day} \times \text{Standard}}{\text{Volume}} = \text{Employees Needed}$

    C. $\dfrac{\text{Hours per man-Day} \times \text{Volume}}{\text{Standard}} = \text{Employees Needed}$

    D. $\dfrac{\text{Volume} \times \text{Standard}}{\text{Hours per man-Day}} = \text{Employees Needed}$

17._____

18. Of the following, which formula is used to determine the number of days required to process work?

    A. $\dfrac{\text{Employees} \times \text{Daily Output}}{\text{Volume}} = \text{Days to Process Work}$

    B. $\dfrac{\text{Employees} \times \text{volume}}{\text{Daily output}} = \text{Days to Process Work}$

    C. $\dfrac{\text{Volume}}{\text{Employees} \times \text{Daily Output}} = \text{Days to Process Work}$

    D. $\dfrac{\text{Volume} \times \text{Daily Output}}{\text{Employees}} = \text{Days to Process Work}$

19. Identify this symbol, as used in a Systems Flow Chart.

    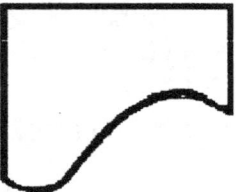

    A. Document B. Decision C. Preparation D. Process

20. Of the following, the MAIN advantage of a form letter over a dictated letter is that a form letter

    A. is more expressive
    B. is neater
    C. may be mailed in a window envelope
    D. requires less secretarial time

21. The term that may be defined as *a systematic analysis of all factors affecting work being done or all factor's that will affect work to be done, in order to save effort, time, or money* is

    A. flow process charting   B. work flow analysis
    C. work measurement   D. work simplification

22. Generally, the LEAST important basic factor to be considered in developing office layout improvements is to locate

    A. office equipment, reference facilities, and files as close as practicable to those using them
    B. persons as close as practicable to the persons from whom they receive their work
    C. persons as close as practicable to windows and/or adequate ventilation
    D. persons who are friendly with each other close together to improve morale

23. Of the following, the one which is LEAST effective in reducing administrative costs is

    A. applying objective measurement techniques to determine the time required to perform a given task
    B. establishing budgets on the basis of historical performance data
    C. motivating supervisors and managers in the importance of cost reduction
    D. selecting the best method -- manual, mechanical, or electronic -- to process the essential work

24. *Fire-fighting* is a common expression in management terminology.
    Of the following, which BEST describes *fire-fighting* as an analyst's approach to solving paperwork problems?

    A. A complete review of all phases of the department's processing functions
    B. A studied determination of the proper equipment to process the work
    C. An analysis of each form that is being processed and the logical reasons for its processing
    D. The solution of problems as they arise, usually at the request of operating personnel

25. Assume that an analyst with a proven record of accomplishment on many projects is having difficulties on his present assignment.
    Of the following, the BEST course of action for his superior to take is to

    A. assume there is a personality conflict involved and transfer the analyst to another project
    B. give the analyst some time off
    C. review the nature of the project to determine whether or not the analyst is equipped to handle the assignment
    D. suggest that the analyst seek counseling

KEY (CORRECT ANSWERS)

1. B
2. D
3. C
4. B
5. D

6. C
7. B
8. A
9. D
10. C

11. A
12. A
13. C
14. C
15. A

16. C
17. D
18. C
19. A
20. D

21. D
22. D
23. B
24. D
25. C

EXAMINATION SECTION
TEST 1

DIRECTIONS: Each question or incomplete statement is followed by several suggested answers or completions. Select the one that BEST answers the question or completes the statement. *PRINT THE LETTER OF THE CORRECT ANSWER IN THE SPACE AT THE RIGHT.*

1. If an analyst recommends to the head of a newly established agency that the latter institute a line type of organization, he should also point out that this structure has the following MAJOR disadvantage:

    A. Delay will be encountered in reaching decisions
    B. Coordination will be difficult to secure
    C. Authority and responsibility will be diffused
    D. Discipline will be hard to maintain

2. Of the following statements which relate to the use of office space, the one that is LEAST valid is:

    A. A request for a conference room on the basis of privacy for meetings usually cannot be justified, for most private offices are suitable for meetings
    B. Private offices are objectionable because they tend to slow up the work by interfering with supervisory effectiveness
    C. The reception room should not handle ordinary and necessary traffic between different areas in the office
    D. The space utilization of private offices is about 35 to 50 percent of that of the open area arrangement

3. In preparing the layout for a small office, PARAMOUNT consideration should be given to a design that will

    A. accommodate the flows representing the largest volumes of work
    B. cause work to progress through its production cycle regardless of backtracking in a straight line or U
    C. increase the speed and movement of papers involved in the flow of work to the shortest compass feasible
    D. take into account vertical relationships of floor locations in the work flow

4. When centralization of office activities is instituted, which one of the following conditions will MOST likely occur?

    A. Confidentiality of office work will decrease.
    B. Equitable wage schedules will be undermined.
    C. Office machine maintenance costs will increase.
    D. Training of office employees will be delayed.

5. Descriptor is a term COMMONLY used in

    A. information retrieval   B. network analysis
    C. planning and forecasting   D. systems analysis

6. Of the following, the BEST way to secure effective management is *usually* to
   A. allow staff agencies to help solve the administrative problems of line management
   B. provide a good organization structure
   C. select capable managers and administrators
   D. set up conservative spans of control

7. The MOST effective way of graphically representing the division of total costs into component costs as they vary over a period of time is by means of a
   A. band chart
   B. pictograph
   C. pie diagram
   D. histogram

8. During the past 50 years, the rate of increase in the number of office workers has been much greater than that of our total working force.
   The LEAST likely reason to cause this increase is the
   A. dispersal of clerical operations which accompanied the growth in manufacturing
   B. development of "service industries"
   C. use of more factual information by managers
   D. expansion in business legislation and governmental regulatory agencies

9. In attempting to discover flaws in an organization, an organization chart has been prepared.
   The condition that will be LEAST likely to be disclosed through use of the organization chart will be
   A. executives who are burdened with details
   B. work schedules that are unmet
   C. promotional possibilities that are not being provided
   D. functions which are becoming secondary due to splitting among departmental units

10. The PRIMARY function of systems analysis in the Planning Programming Budgetary System is to
    A. cost out various alternatives
    B. develop a PERT chart for evaluating program content
    C. develop better alternatives than those which are in the currently approved program
    D. provide perspective in judging the validity of an expenditure

11. Systems analysis would be LEAST effective in solving which of these problems? The
    A. determination of need for a new pier
    B. problem of air pollution
    C. selection of a site for a police station
    D. selection of engineering personnel

12. In procedural analysis, when the purpose of a particular step has been shown to be justifiable to the end purpose of the procedure, the NEXT necessary step is, usually, to
    A. determine the time limits for the step
    B. weigh the value of the step against the expense involved
    C. sell the idea to the supervisory staff
    D. make it a part of the procedure

13. ▽ is a symbol used in records management flow diagrams to indicate

   A. destruction of paper
   B. filing and/or permanent storage
   C. inspection
   D. microfilming is necessary

14. The concept that decisions should be made at the lowest level in an organization where all the (required) information and competence are available is MOST particularly a general rule in

   A. communications theory
   B. decentralization of authority
   C. incremental decision-making
   D. span of control

15. An office quality control program may comprise several approaches.
The one LEAST desirable of the following normally is to

   A. follow a policy of spot or sample checking
   B. follow a practice of 100% checking of all work to verify its correctness
   C. inspect the work by means of a statistical quality control program
   D. review and tally errors being detected from present checking operations to determine the amount of checking presently being followed and the results being obtained

16. When a form is to be completed by an electronic data processing machine, which of the following is LEAST necessary?

   A. Form number
   B. Form title
   C. Lines
   D. Margins

17. Under a PPBS system, the selection of the proper alternative program should be made by the

   A. administrator responsible for the program, with the approval of the mayor and city legislative body
   B. budget director, basing his decision according to the optimum alternative
   C. budget examiner who reviews the administration budget
   D. chief systems analyst who programmed the alternatives

18. Which of the following is LEAST applicable in describing PPBS as a general concept? A

   A. quantitative method of budgeting for the coming year
   B. system of defining long-range alternative programs and planning the allocation of resources on the basis of the cost of the long-range program versus the benefit derived over the planning period
   C. system of measuring budgeted performance against pre-established goals
   D. system that establishes the importance of a program in terms of the expected cost of executing it

19. Under a PPBS system, substantive planning is NORMALLY defined as

    A. fiscal planning
    B. planning of future budgets
    C. planning of objectives-ultimate and intermediate
    D. planning of programs-ultimate and intermediate

20. The method of selection which would provide the TIGHTEST standard under the logging method of work measurement would be

    A. one-third array
    B. modal average
    C. selected arithmetic average
    D. upper quartile

21. A concept for the evaluation of managers whereby goals are set and agreed upon for each manager, and then his attainment of those goals is evaluated at a particular prearranged target date, is BEST termed

    A. management by objectives
    B. management evaluation planning
    C. managerial performance appraisal
    D. program evaluation

22. When work is organized so that the work is broken into a series of jobs, and each unit of work (a customer order, invoice, etc.) moves progressively from position to position until completion, we would NORMALLY refer to this as the

    A. parallel plan of work subdivision
    B. serial plan
    C. unit assembly plan
    D. unit process plan

23. The type of organization in which employees report to a nominal manager for administrative purposes but are assigned to *ad hoc* supervisors as various assignments arise is BEST termed the _____ type of organization.

    A. functional
    B. process
    C. project or task force
    D. unit assembly

24. The expression which BEST defines a generalized situation in which several programs may be executed simultaneously or concurrently is

    A. multiprocessing
    B. multiprogramming
    C. on-line, real time programming
    D. process overlap

25. The sampling technique which consists of taking selections at constant intervals (every nth unit) from a list of the universe is called _____ sampling.

    A. area
    B. quota
    C. stratified random
    D. systematic

26. A method of project scheduling and control which shows the MOST optimistic, MOST pessimistic, and MOST probable estimate of time for how long each task in a project will take is called

    A. CPM (Critical Path Method)
    B. Gantt charting
    C. Linear Responsibility Charting
    D. PERT

27. The idea that classic organizational structure tends to create work situations having requirements counter to those for psychological success and self-esteem, sometimes called the "organizational dilemma", is MOST closely associated with which one of the following persons?

    A. Chris Argyris   B. Frederick Taylor
    C. Luther Gulick   D. Max Weber

28. Charles J. Hitch is known PRIMARILY for his work in the area of

    A. administrative behavior B. behavioral sciences
    C. organizational analysis D. PPBS

Questions 29-30.

DIRECTIONS: Questions 29 and 30 relate to the paragraph below.

If one were to observe the information, in all its variant forms, that flows to a manager in the typical American enterprise, he would have a word for it: chaos. Subordinates want to be helpful, or to promote themselves, or to reflect discredit somewhere, and they originate or serve as a transmission belt for information they think the manager should have. Furthermore, it is the nature of the business process that information is generated where it is most easily reflected and is very scarce in areas or phases where data are not readily available. If one could project a tape which showed information density through time, he would find areas of heavy concentration and areas of little or no cloudiness. This means two things: First, people seem to have an inner drive to report available information in many ways, many forms, and for many users. Note what an accountant or statistician can do with two figures—or a mathematician without any figures at all! Second, the lack of information in specific areas means only that it is not available; it does not mean that it is unnecessary. Indeed, the blind areas may be of the greatest importance for decision-making purposes.

29. The result of the state of affairs described in the above paragraph would MOST likely be

    A. inconsequential
    B. an impetus to proper decision-making
    C. high costs and poor decisions
    D. a successful uniform information system

30. The author in this paragraph is PRIMARILY concerned with

    A. decision-making theory
    B. communications
    C. tape information systems
    D. information gathering by accountants and statisticians

KEY (CORRECT ANSWERS)

1. B	11. D	21. A
2. A	12. B	22. B
3. A	13. B	23. C
4. A	14. B	24. B
5. A	15. B	25. D
6. C	16. C	26. D
7. A	17. A	27. A
8. A	18. A	28. D
9. B	19. C	29. C
10. C	20. D	30. B

TEST 2

DIRECTIONS: Each question or incomplete statement is followed by several suggested answers or completions. Select the one that BEST answers the question or completes the statement. *PRINT THE LETTER OF THE CORRECT ANSWER IN THE SPACE AT THE RIGHT.*

1. It has been decided to make a few important revisions in the methods and procedures of a particular work unit. Of the following, the method of implementing these revisions which would probably be MOST desirable in terms of morale as well as efficiency is to

    A. give all the employees in the work unit individual instructions in the revised procedures, making sure that each employee fully understands the changes before instructing the next employee
    B. institute all the revisions at once, followed by on-the-job training for all the employees in the work unit
    C. introduce the revisions one at a time, accompanying each revision with an orientation for the employees
    D. set up a training course for the employees, instructing them in all aspects of the revised procedures prior to their implementation

2. In an administrative survey of a multiple-unit organization, which of the following is it usually MOST important to identify? The

    A. data and information used commonly by units, how used and by whom
    B. flow of data and information within a single organization unit
    C. type and volume of data used within individual units and transmitted between units
    D. way data and information are transmitted between units, how used and by whom

3. A noted authority has described a common method of making organizational policy in which the decision-maker tries to find some acceptable level of goal accomplishment short of ultimate fulfillment of all objectives and to frame policies toward such fulfillment. Of the following, this method is BEST termed

    A. feedback
    C. satisfying
    B. incrementalism
    D. seriality

4. The managerial grid, as defined by Blake and Mouton, shows two concerns and a range of interaction between them as follows: The horizontal axis indicates a concern for

    A. hierarchy, while the vertical axis indicates a concern for people
    B. production, while the vertical axis indicates a concern for people
    C. organization, while the vertical axis indicates a concern for people
    D. people, while the vertical axis indicates a concern for P/L (profit or loss)

5. In the managerial grid, which managerial style is dominant for any given person in any particular situation can be determined by any one or several sets of conditions in combination. The five conditions in CORRECT order are:

    A. Organization, management, values, chance, production
    B. Organization, situation, values, personality, chance
    C. Production, situation, personality, chance, individuality
    D. Values, personality, variety, organization, chance

6. The analyst may be faced with a choice of either recommending service contracts or recommending on-call service for maintenance of equipment.
   In making a decision, the one of the following factors which would mitigate MOST against the use of on-call service would be that

   A. equipment utilization is not heavy
   B. prompt service when breakdowns occur is seldom essential
   C. regular checkups and servicing are considered desirable based on past equipment history
   D. trade-ins are made frequently

7. The type of paper stock MOST commonly used for office forms work is _____ bond.

   A. cotton content
   B. duplicating or mimeo
   C. rag
   D. sulphite

8. In laying out an office, according to most authorities, the amount of space which NORMALLY should be allowed for a clerk would be in the range of _____ square feet.

   A. 10 to 15
   B. 25 to 100
   C. 110 to 125
   D. 130 to 150

9. A noted behavioral scientist believes that the MOST important element in job satisfaction, of those listed below, is

   A. job security
   B. responsibility or recognition
   C. salary
   D. type of supervision

10. The point of view that the average human being prefers to be directed, wishes to avoid responsibility, has relatively little ambition, and wants security above all has been described in Douglas MacGregor's classic book on human motivation in business.
    He includes this point of view in what he calls

    A. Theory X
    B. Theory Y
    C. Theory Z
    D. Theory X and Y combined

11. New desk top electronic machines are of two main types-printing or display. Display type machines show the results by any of the following methods EXCEPT for

    A. cathode ray tube
    B. electro-mechanical
    C. mosaic or liquid crystal
    D. nixie

12. The type of chart that is normally MOST useful for studying the work assignments and job content of individual positions in a particular organizational unit when making a procedure analysis is the _____ chart.

    A. columnar flow
    B. procedure flow
    C. work distribution
    D. work process

13. To prepare a work distribution chart, two other types of lists generally must be prepared. In the usual order of preparation, they are FIRST a(n)

    A. flow diagram, then an activity list
    B. skills list, then a task list
    C. task list, then an activity list
    D. activity list, then a task list

14. The critical path is defined as that path (or those paths) through a network

    A. showing the least number of time units
    B. showing the greatest number of time units
    C. which consists (or consist) entirely of sequential activities
    D. which links (or link) together activities in concurrent relationship to each other

15. A statistical quality control program in the office is valuable in alerting management that the level of quality for particular transactions has deteriorated. It is, however, LEAST likely to reveal

    A. when preventive action is necessary
    B. when a variation is due to other than chance
    C. when an assignable cause is present
    D. what the cause of the error is

16. In work measurement, the value of a TMU is _____ min.

    A. .0001   B. .0006   C. .0036   D. .0100

17. The sheet version of microfilm is NORMALLY referred to as

    A. microfiche   B. micro-sheet
    C. microdupe   D. microspec

18. While a line and staff organization is generally considered to have the advantages of both a line organization and a functional organization, with the disadvantages of each eliminated, disadvantages nevertheless, do exist.
    Of the following, the one that describes the MOST significant disadvantage of a line and staff type of organization is that

    A. fewer opportunities are afforded to match the capacities of personnel with the job, since a smaller number of jobs is required
    B. line orders and staff advice, although clearly known to managers, tend to be confused by non-management members
    C. staff officers may attempt to take over line authority
    D. staff officers may tend to follow the ideas of the line officers and not generate their own ideas

19. Which activities take the most time? Are skills being utilized properly? Are employees doing too many unrelated tasks?
    Of the following, the BEST technique to find answers to all of these questions is the

    A. flow diagram   B. skills chart
    C. work count   D. work distribution chart

20. Operator participation in management improvement work is LEAST likely to do which one of the following?

    A. Assure the use of the best available management techniques.
    B. Make installation of new procedures quicker and easier.
    C. Overcome the stigma of the outside expert.
    D. Take advantage of the desire of most operators to seek self-improvement.

21. Which of the following BEST defines an organization chart? A

    A. chart depicting the informal channels of communications within an organization
    B. chart depicting the major functions of an organization and the normal work flow between subdivisions of the organization
    C. graphic presentation of the arrangement and interrelationships of the subdivisions and functions of an organization as they exist
    D. graphic presentation of the arrangement and relationships of all positions authorized in an organization

22. Under a PPBS system, fiscal planning is NORMALLY considered to be planning

    A. for anticipated fixed costs only
    B. for present personnel requirements, procurement, and construction
    C. of current income and expenditures
    D. of future budgets

23. In the selection of space within an office building, LEAST consideration, generally, should be given to which of the following factors?

    A. Future expansion
    B. Proximity to elevators and restrooms
    C. Stability of other tenants on other floors
    D. Ventilation

24. In office layout, an office unit consisting of a combined desk and file cabinet and small movable partitions may BEST be described as _____ unit.

    A. conference   B. landscaped office
    C. modular office   D. semi-private office

25. Which of the following is it generally MOST important to consider when allocating office space?

    A. Actual organizational relationships
    B. Lighting requirements
    C. Noise levels
    D. Preferences of employees with over ten years of seniority

26. In preparing office layouts, the one of the following general factors within the affected unit which should generally receive the LEAST consideration is

    A. lighting levels in the existing area
    B. major work flow–the processing of paper
    C. present and projected growth rate of the unit
    D. traffic patterns of employees and visitors

27. In reviewing a new office layout, the one of the following questions that should normally receive LEAST consideration is:

    A. Have several alternate move day plans been prepared showing possible new locations of each piece of office equipment?
    B. Has expansion been provided for?
    C. Have alternate schemes been adequately explored to try to achieve the best possible layout?
    D. Is there adequate aisle space for ingress and egress?

28. Which of the following is the LEAST important reason for preparing a written study report? The

    A. report documents findings and recommendations so that the client can review and comment on them
    B. report is of interest as an historical document
    C. report serves as a document useful in implementing the recommendations
    D. writing process itself helps the analyst structure his thinking and conclusions

29. According to the classic studies by Rensis Likert at the University of Michigan, the GREATEST factor making for good morale and increased productivity was having a

    A. good program of employee benefits and wage scales
    B. supervisor who gave his employees free rein, after they were fully trained, and did not interfere with them
    C. supervisor who was interested primarily in production
    D. supervisor who, while also interested in production, was primarily "employee-centered"

30. Organization structure deals with the relationship of functions and the personnel performing these functions. It is usually advisable to think first of functions, then of the individuals performing these functions.
    MOST implicit in this approach is the recognition that

    A. conditions outside the organization may necessitate changes in the organization structure
    B. functions need not always be coordinated for an organization to effectively carry out its objectives
    C. functions tend to change with time while the interests and abilities of personnel are usually permanent
    D. personnel emphasis often results in unusual combinations of duties that are difficult to manage

KEY (CORRECT ANSWERS)

1. D	11. B	21. C
2. A	12. C	22. D
3. C	13. C	23. C
4. B	14. A	24. C
5. B	15. D	25. A
6. C	16. B	26. A
7. D	17. A	27. A
8. B	18. C	28. B
9. B	19. D	29. D
10. A	20. A	30. D

———

EXAMINATION SECTION
TEST 1

DIRECTIONS: Each question or incomplete statement is followed by several suggested answers or completions. Select the one that BEST answers the question or completes the statement. *PRINT THE LETTER OF THE CORRECT ANSWER IN THE SPACE AT THE RIGHT.*

1. A management approach widely used today is based on the belief that decisions should be made and actions should be taken by managers closest to the organization's problems.
   This style of management is MOST appropriately called _____ management.

   A. scientific
   B. means-end
   C. decentralized
   D. internal process

2. As contrasted with tall organization structures with narrow spans of control, flat organization structures with wide spans of control MOST usually provide

   A. fast communication and information flows
   B. more levels in the organizational hierarchy
   C. fewer workers reporting to supervisors
   D. lower motivation because of tighter control standards

3. Use of the systems approach is MOST likely to lead to

   A. consideration of the impact on the whole organization of actions taken in any part of that organization
   B. the placing of restrictions on departmental authority
   C. use of mathematical models to suboptimize production
   D. consideration of the activities of each unit of an organization as a totality without regard to the remainder of the organization

4. An administrator, with overall responsibility for all administrative operations in a large operating agency, is considering organizing the agency's personnel office around either of the following two alternative concepts:
   Alternative I- a corps of specialists for each branch of personnel subject matter, whose skills, counsel, or work products are coordinated only by the agency personnel officer
   Alternative II- a crew of so-called *personnel generalists*, who individually work with particular segments of the organization but deal with all subspecialties of the personnel function
   The one of the following which MOST tends to be a DRAWBACK of Alternative I, as compared with Alternative II, is that

   A. training and employee relations work call for education, interests, and talents that differ from those required for classification and compensation work
   B. personnel office staff may develop only superficial familiarity with the specialized areas to which they have been assigned
   C. supervisors may fail to get continuing overall personnel advice on an integrated basis
   D. the personnel specialists are likely to become so interested in and identified with the operating view as to particular cases that they lose their professional objectivity and become merely advocates of what some supervisor wants

5. The matrix summary or decision matrix is a useful tool for making choices. Its effectiveness is MOST dependent upon the user's ability to

   A. write a computer program (Fortran or Cobol)
   B. assign weights representing the relative importance of the objectives
   C. solve a set of two equations with two unknowns
   D. work with matrix algebra

6. An organizational form which is set up only on an *ad hoc* basis to meet specific goals is said PRIMARILY to use

   A. clean break departmentation
   B. matrix or task force organization
   C. scalar specialization
   D. geographic or area-wide decentralization

7. The concept of job enlargement would LEAST properly be implemented by

   A. permitting workers to follow through on tasks or projects from start to finish
   B. delegating the maximum authority possible for decision-making to lower levels in the hierarchy
   C. maximizing the number of professional classes in the classification plan
   D. training employees to grow beyond whatever tasks they have been performing

8. As used in the area of administration, the principle of *unity of command* MOST specifically means that

   A. an individual should report to only one superior for any single activity
   B. individuals make better decisions than do committees
   C. in large organizations, chains of command are normally too long
   D. an individual should not supervise over five subordinates

9. The methods of operations research, statistical decision-making, and linear programming have been referred to as the tool kit of the manager.
   Utilization of these tools is LEAST useful in the performance of which of the following functions?

   A. Elimination of the need for using judgment when making decisions
   B. Facilitation of decision-making without the need for sub-optimization
   C. Quantifying problems for management study
   D. Research and analysis of management operations

10. When acting in their respective managerial capacities, the chief executive officer and the office supervisor both perform the fundamental functions of management. Of the following differences between the two, the one which is generally considered to be the LEAST significant is the

    A. breadth of the objectives
    B. complexity of measuring actual efficiency of performance
    C. number of decisions made
    D. organizational relationships affected by actions taken

11. The ability of operations researchers to solve complicated problems rests on their use of models.
    These models can BEST be described as

    A. mathematical statements of the problem
    B. physical constructs that simulate a work layout
    C. toy-like representations of employees in work environments
    D. role-playing simulations

12. Of the following, it is MOST likely to be proper for the agency head to allow the agency personnel officer to make final selection of appointees from certified eligible lists where there are

    A. *small* numbers of employees to be hired in newly-developed professional fields
    B. *large* numbers of persons to be hired for key managerial positions
    C. *large* numbers of persons to be hired in very routine occupations where the individual discretion of operating officials is not vital
    D. *small* numbers of persons to be hired in highly specialized professional occupations which are vital to the agency's operations

13. Of the following, an operating agency personnel office is LEAST likely to be able to exert strong influence or control within the operating agency by

    A. interpreting to the operating agency head what is intended by the directives and rules emanating from the central personnel agency
    B. establishing the key objectives of those line divisions of the operating agency employing large numbers of staff and operating under the management-by-objectives approach
    C. formulating and proposing to the agency head the internal policies and procedures on personnel matters required within the operating agency
    D. exercising certain discretionary authority in the application of the agency head's general personnel policies to actual specific situations

14. PERT is a recently developed system used *primarily* to

    A. evaluate the quality of applicants' backgrounds
    B. analyze and control the timing aspects of a major project
    C. control the total expenditure of agency funds within a monthly or quarterly time period
    D. analyze and control the differential effect on costs of purchasing in different quantities

15. Assume that an operating agency has among its vacant positions two positions, each of which encompasses mixed duties. Both require appointees to have considerable education and experience, but these requirements are essential only for the more difficult duties of these positions. In the place of these positions, an administrator creates two new positions, one in which the higher duties are concentrated and the other with the lesser functions requiring only minimum preparation.
    Of the following, it is generally MOST appropriate to characterize the administrator's action as a(n)

A. *undesirable* example of deliberate downgrading of standards and requirements
B. *undesirable* manipulation of the classification system for non-merit purposes
C. *desirable* broadening of the definition of a class of positions
D. *desirable* example of job redesign

16. Of the following, the LEAST important stumbling block to the development of personnel mobility among governmental jurisdictions is the

    A. limitations on lateral entry above junior levels in many jurisdictions
    B. continued collection of filing fees for civil service tests by many governmental jurisdictions
    C. absence of reciprocal exchange of retirement benefit eligibility between governments
    D. disparities in salary scales between governments

17. Of the following, the MAJOR disadvantage of a personnel system that features the *selection out* (forced retirement) of those who have been passed over a number of times for promotion is that such a system

    A. wastes manpower which is perfectly competent at one level but unable to rise above that level
    B. wastes funds by requiring review boards
    C. leads to excessive recruiting of newcomers from outside the system
    D. may not be utilized in *closed* career systems with low maximum age limits for entrance

18. Of the following, the fields in which operating agency personnel offices generally exercise the MOST stringent controls over first line supervisors in the agency are

    A. methods analysis and work simplification
    B. selection and position classification
    C. vestibule training and Gantt chart
    D. suggestion systems and staff development

19. Of the following, computers are normally MOST effective in handling

    A. large masses of data requiring simple processing
    B. small amounts of data requiring constantly changing complex processing
    C. data for which reported values are often subject to inaccuracies
    D. large amounts of data requiring continual programming and reprocessing

20. Contingency planning, which has long been used by the military and is assuming increasing importance in other organizations, may BEST be described as a process which utilizes

    A. alternative plans based on varying assumptions
    B. *crash programs* by organizations departmentalized along process lines
    C. plans which mandate substitution of equipment for manpower at predetermined operational levels
    D. plans that individually and accurately predict future events

21. In the management of inventory, two kinds of costs normally determine when to order and in what amounts. The one of the following choices which includes BOTH of these kinds of costs is _____ costs and _____ costs.

    A. carrying; storage
    B. personnel; order
    C. computer; order
    D. personnel; computer

22. At top management levels, the one of the following which is generally the MOST important executive skill is skill in

    A. budgeting procedures
    B. a technical discipline
    C. controlling actions in accordance with previously approved plans
    D. seeing the organization as a whole

23. Of the following, the BEST way to facilitate the successful operation of a committee is to set guidelines establishing its

    A. budget exclusive of personnel costs
    B. location
    C. schedule of meetings or conferences
    D. scope or purpose

24. Executive training programs that single out particular managers and groom them for promotion create the so-called organizational *crown princes.*
    Of the following, the MOST serious problem that arises in connection with this practice is that

    A. the managers chosen for promotion seldom turn out to be the best managers since the future potential of persons cannot be predicted
    B. not enough effort is made to remove organizational obstacles in the way of their development and achievement
    C. the resentment of the managers not selected for the program has an adverse effect on the motivation of those managers not selected
    D. performance appraisal and review are not carried out systematically enough

25. Of the following, the LEAST likely result of the use of the concept of job enlargement is that

    A. coordination will be simplified
    B. the individual's job will become less challenging
    C. worker satisfaction will increase
    D. fewer people will have to give attention to each piece of work

KEY (CORRECT ANSWERS)

1. C
2. A
3. A
4. C
5. B

6. B
7. C
8. A
9. A
10. C

11. A
12. C
13. B
14. B
15. D

16. B
17. A
18. B
19. A
20. A

21. A
22. D
23. D
24. C
25. B

TEST 2

DIRECTIONS: Each question or incomplete statement is followed by several suggested answers or completions. Select the one that BEST answers the question or completes the statement. *PRINT THE LETTER OF THE CORRECT ANSWER IN THE SPACE AT THE RIGHT.*

1. The one of the following which is MOST likely to be emphasized in the use of the brainstorming technique is the

    A. early consideration of cost factors of all ideas which may be suggested
    B. avoidance of impractical suggestions
    C. separation of the generation of ideas from their evaluation
    D. appraisal of suggestions concurrently with their initial presentation

    1.____

2. Of the following, the BEST method for assessing managerial performance is generally to

    A. compare the manager's accomplishments against clear, specific, agreed-upon goals
    B. compare the manager's traits with those of his peers on a predetermined objective scale
    C. measure the manager's behavior against a listing of itemized personal traits
    D. measure the manager's success according to the enumeration of the *satisfaction* principle

    2.____

3. As compared with recruitment from outside, selection from within the service must generally show GREATER concern for the

    A. prestige in which the public service as a whole is held by the public
    B. morale of the candidate group comprising the recruitment field
    C. cost of examining per candidate
    D. benefits of the use of standardized and validated tests

    3.____

4. Performance budgeting focuses PRIMARY attention upon which one of the following? The

    A. things to be acquired, such as supplies and equipment
    B. general character and relative importance of the work to be done or the service to be rendered
    C. list of personnel to be employed, by specific title
    D. separation of employee performance evaluations from employee compensation

    4.____

5. Of the following, the FIRST step in the installation and operation of a performance budgeting system generally should be the

    A. identification of program costs in relationship to the accounting system and operating structure
    B. identification of the specific end results of past programs in other jurisdictions
    C. identification of work programs that are meaningful for management purposes
    D. establishment of organizational structures each containing only one work program

    5.____

6. Of the following, the MOST important purpose of a system of quarterly allotments of appropriated funds generally is to enable the

   A. head of the judicial branch to determine the legality of agency requests for budget increases
   B. operating agencies of government to upgrade the quality of their services without increasing costs
   C. head of the executive branch to control the rate at which the operating agencies obligate and expend funds
   D. operating agencies of government to avoid payment for services which have not been properly rendered by employees

7. In the preparation of the agency's budget, the agency's central budget office has two responsibilities: program review and management improvement.
   Which one of the following questions concerning an operating agency's program is MOST closely related to the agency budget officer's program review responsibility?

   A. Can expenditures for supplies, materials, or equipment be reduced?
   B. Will improved work methods contribute to a more effective program?
   C. What is the relative importance of this program as compared with other programs?
   D. Will a realignment of responsibilities contribute to a higher level of program performance?

8. Of the following, the method of evaluating relative rates of return normally and generally thought to be MOST useful in evaluating government operations is _____ analysis.

   A. cost-benefit
   B. budget variance
   C. investment capital
   D. budget planning program

9. The one of the following assumptions that is LEAST likely to be made by a democratic or permissive type of leader is that

   A. commitment to goals is seldom a result of monetary rewards alone
   B. people can learn not only to accept, but also to seek, responsibility
   C. the average person prefers security over advancement
   D. creativity may be found in most segments of the population

10. In attempting to motivate subordinates, a manager should PRINCIPALLY be aware of the fact that

    A. the psychological qualities of people, in general, are easily predictable
    B. fear, as a traditional form of motivation, has lost much of its former power to motivate people in our modern industrial society
    C. fear is still the most potent force in motivating the behavior of subordinates in the public service
    D. the worker has very little control over the quality and quantity of his output

11. Assume that the following figures represent the number of work-units that were produced during a week by each of sixteen employees in a division:

    | 12 | 16 | 13 | 18 |
    | 21 | 12 | 16 | 13 |
    | 16 | 13 | 17 | 21 |
    | 13 | 15 | 18 | 20 |

    If all of the employees of the division who produced thirteen work-units during the week had instead produced fifteen work-units during that same week, then for that week, the

    A. mean, median, and mode would all change
    B. mean and mode would change, but the median would remain the same
    C. mode and median would change, but the mean would remain the same
    D. mode, mean, and median would all still remain unchanged in value

12. An important law in motivation theory is called the *law of effect*. This law says that behavior which satisfies a person's needs tends to be repeated; behavior which does not satisfy a person's needs tends to be eliminated. The one of the following which is the BEST interpretation of this law is that

    A. productivity depends on personality traits
    B. diversity of goals leads to instability of motivation
    C. the greater the satisfaction, the more likely it is that the behavior will be reinforced
    D. extrinsic satisfaction is more important than intrinsic reward

13. Of the following, the MOST acceptable reason an administrator can give for taking advice from other employees in the organization only when he asks for it is that he wants to

    A. encourage creativity and high morale
    B. keep dysfunctional pressures and inconsistent recommendations to a minimum
    C. show his superiors and peers who is in charge
    D. show his subordinates who is in charge

14. A complete picture of the communication channels in an organization can BEST be revealed by

    A. observing the planned paperwork system
    B. recording the highly intermittent patterns of communication
    C. plotting the entire flow of information over a period of time
    D. monitoring the *grapevine*

Questions 15-16.

DIRECTIONS: Answer Questions 15 and 16 SOLELY on the basis of the passage below.

Management by objectives (MBO) may be defined as the process by which the superior and the subordinate managers of an organization jointly define its common goals, define each individual's major areas of responsibility in terms of the results expected of him and use these measures as guides for operating the unit and assessing the contribution of each of its members.

The MBO approach requires that after organizational goals are established and communicated, targets must be set for each individual position which are congruent with organizational goals. Periodic performance reviews and a final review using the objectives set as criteria are also basic to this approach.

Recent studies have shown that MBO programs are influenced by attitudes and perceptions of the boss, the company, the reward-punishment system, and the program itself. In addition, the manner in which the MBO program is carried out can influence the success of the program. A study done in the late sixties indicates that the best results are obtained when the manager sets goals which deal with significant problem areas in the organizational unit, or with the subordinate's personal deficiencies. These goals must be clear with regard to what is expected of the subordinate. The frequency of feedback is also important in the success of a management-by-Objectives program. Generally, the greater the amount of feedback, the more successful the MBO program.

15. According to the above passage, the expected output for individual employees should be determined

    A. after a number of reviews of work performance
    B. after common organizational goals are defined
    C. before common organizational goals are defined
    D. on the basis of an employee's personal qualities

16. According to the above passage, the management-by-objectives approach requires

    A. less feedback than other types of management programs
    B. little review of on-the-job performance after the initial setting of goals
    C. general conformance between individual goals and organizational goals
    D. the setting of goals which deal with minor problem areas in the organization

Questions 17-19.

DIRECTIONS: Answer Questions 17 to 19 SOLELY on the basis of the passage below.

During the last decade, a great deal of interest has been generated around the phenomenon of organizational development, or the process of developing human resources through conscious organisation effort. Organizational development (OD) stresses improving interpersonal relationships and organizational skills, such as communication, to a much greater degree than individual training ever did.

The kind of training that an organization should emphasize depends upon the present and future structure of the organization. If future organizations are to be unstable, shifting coalitions, then individual skills and abilities, particularly those emphasizing innovativeness, creativity, flexibility, and the latest technological knowledge, are crucial, and individual training is most appropriate.

But if there is to be little change in organizational structure, then the main thrust of training should be group-oriented or organizational development. This approach seems better designed for overcoming hierarchical barriers, for developing a degree of interpersonal relationships which make communication along the chain of command possible, and for retaining a modicum of innovation and/or flexibility.

17. According to the above passage, group-oriented training is MOST useful in

    A. developing a communications system that will facilitate understanding through the chain of command
    B. highly flexible and mobile organizations
    C. preventing the crossing of hierarchical barriers within an organization
    D. saving energy otherwise wasted on developing methods of dealing with rigid hierarchies

18. The one of the following conclusions which can be drawn MOST appropriately from the above passage is that

    A. behavioral research supports the use of organizational development training methods rather than individualized training
    B. it is easier to provide individualized training in specific skills than to set up sensitivity training programs
    C. organizational development eliminates innovative or flexible activity
    D. the nature of an organization greatly influences which training methods will be most effective

19. According to the above passage, the one of the following which is LEAST important for large-scale organizations geared to rapid and abrupt change is

    A. current technological information
    B. development of a high degree of interpersonal relationships
    C. development of individual skills and abilities
    D. emphasis on creativity

Questions 20-25.

DIRECTIONS: Each of Questions 20 through 25 consists of a statement which contains one word that is incorrectly used because it is not in keeping with the meaning that the quotation is evidently intended to convey. Determine which word is INCORRECTLY used. Select from the choices lettered A, B, C, and D the word which, when substituted for the incorrectly used word, would BEST help to convey the meaning of the statement.

20. One of the considerations likely to affect the currency of classification, particularly in professional and managerial occupations, is the impact of the incumbent's capacities on the job. Some work is highly susceptible to change as the result of the special talents or interests of the classifier. Organization should never be so rigid as not to capitalize on the innovative or unusual proclivities of its key employees. While a machine operator may not be able, even subtly, to change the character or level of his job, the design engineer, the attorney, or the organization and methods analyst might readily do so. Reliance on his judgment and the scope of his assignments may both grow as the result of his skill, insight, and capacity.

    A. unlikely   B. incumbent   C. directly   D. scope

20.____

21. The supply of services by the state is not governed by market price. The aim is to supply such services to all who need them and to treat all consumers equally. This objective especially compels the civil servant to maintain a role of strict impartiality, based on the principle of equality of individual citizens vis-a-vis their government. However, there is a clear difference between being neutral and being impartial. If the requirement is construed to mean that all civil servants should be political eunuchs, devoid of the drive and motivation essential to dynamic administration, then the concept of impartiality is being seriously utilized. Modern governments should not be stopped from demanding that their hirelings have not only the technical but the emotional qualifications necessary for wholehearted effort.

    A. determined   B. rule   C. stable   D. misapplied

21.____

22. The manager was barely listening. Recently, at the divisional level, several new fronts of troubles had erupted, including a requirement to increase production yet hold down operating costs and somehow raise quality standards. Though the three objectives were basically obsolete, top departmental management was insisting on the simultaneous attainment of them, an insistence not helping the manager's ulcer, an old enemy within. Thus, the manager could not find time for interest in individuals-only in statistics which regiments of individuals, like unconsidered Army privates, added up to.

    A. quantity   B. battalion   C. incompatible   D. quiet

22.____

23. When a large volume of data flows directly between operators and first-line supervisors, senior executives tend to be out of the mainstream of work. Summary reports can increase their remoteness. An executive needs to know the volume, quality, and cost of completed work, and exceptional problems. In addition, he may desire information on key operating conditions. Summary reports on these matters are, therefore, essential features of a communications network and make delegation without loss of control possible.

    A. unimportant   B. quantity
    C. offset   D. incomplete

23.____

24. Of major significance in management is harmony between the overall objectives of the organization and the managerial objectives within that organization. In addition, harmony among goals of managers is impossible; they should not be at cross-purposes. Each manager's goal should supplement and assist the goals of his colleagues. Likewise, the objectives of individuals or nonmanagement members should be harmonized with those of the manager. When this is accomplished, genuine teamwork is the result, and human relations are aided materially. The integration of managers' and individuals' goals aids in achieving greater work satisfaction at all levels.   24.____

    A. competition
    B. dominate
    C. incremental
    D. vital

25. Change constantly challenges the manager. Some of this change is evolutionary, some revolutionary, some recognizable, some nonrecognizable. Both forces within an enterprise and forces outside the enterprise cause managers to act and react in initiating changes in their immediate working environment. Change invalidates existing operations. Goals are not being accomplished in the best manner, problems develop, and frequently because of the lack of time, only patched-up solutions are followed. The result is that the mode of management is profound in nature and temporary in effectiveness. A complete overhaul of managerial operations should take place. It appears quite likely that we are just beginning to see the real effects of change in our society; the pace probably will accelerate in ways that few really understand or know how to handle.   25.____

    A. confirms
    B. decline
    C. instituting
    D. superficial

KEY (CORRECT ANSWERS)

1.	C	11.	B
2.	A	12.	C
3.	B	13.	B
4.	B	14.	C
5.	C	15.	B
6.	C	16.	C
7.	C	17.	A
8.	A	18.	D
9.	C	19.	B
10.	B	20.	B

21. D
22. C
23. C
24. D
25. D

EXAMINATION SECTION
TEST 1

DIRECTIONS: Each question or incomplete statement is followed by several suggested answers or completions. Select the one that BEST answers the question or completes the statement. *PRINT THE LETTER OF THE CORRECT ANSWER IN THE SPACE AT THE RIGHT.*

1. Assume that a manager is preparing a list of reasons to justify making a major change in methods and procedures in his agency.
   Which of the following reasons would be LEAST appropriate on such a list?

   A. Improve the means for satisfying needs and wants of agency personnel
   B. Increase efficiency
   C. Intensify competition and stimulate loyalty to separate work groups
   D. Contribute to the individual and group satisfaction of agency personnel

2. Many managers recognize the benefits of decentralization but are concerned about the danger of over-relaxation of control as a result of increased delegation.
   Of the following, the MOST appropriate means of establishing proper control under decentralization is for the manager to

   A. establish detailed standards for all phases of operation
   B. shift his attention from operating details to appraisal of results
   C. keep himself informed by decreasing the time span covered by reports
   D. make unilateral decisions on difficult situations that arise in decentralized locations

3. In some agencies, the counsel to the agency head is given the right to bypass the chain of command and issue orders directly to the staff concerning matters that involve certain specific processes and practices.
   This situation MOST NEARLY illustrates the principle of

   A. the acceptance theory of authority
   B. multiple-linear authority
   C. splintered authority
   D. functional authority

4. Assume that a manager is writing a brief report to his superior outlining the advantages of matrix organization. Of the following, it would be INCORRECT to state that

   A. in matrix organization, a project is emphasized by designating one individual as the focal point for all matters pertaining to it
   B. utilization of manpower can be flexible in matrix organization because a reservoir of specialists is maintained in the line operations
   C. the usual line staff arrangement is generally reversed in matrix organization
   D. in matrix organization, responsiveness to project needs is generally faster due to establishing needed communication lines and decision points

5. It is commonly understood that communication is an important part of the administrative process.
Which of the following is NOT a valid principle of the communication process in administration?

   A. The channels of communication should be spontaneous.
   B. The lines of communication should be as direct and as short as possible.
   C. Communications should be authenticated.
   D. The persons serving in communications centers should be competent.

6. The PRIMARY purpose of the quantitative approach in management is to

   A. identify better alternatives for management decision-making
   B. substitute data for judgment
   C. match opinions to data
   D. match data to opinions

7. If an executive wants to make a strong case for running his agency as a flat type of structure, he should point out that the PRIMARY advantage of doing so is to

   A. provide less experience in decision-making for agency personnel
   B. facilitate frequent contact between each superior and his immediate subordinates
   C. improve communication and unify attitudes
   D. improve communication and diversify attitudes

8. In deciding how detailed his delegation of authority to a subordinate should be, a manager should follow the general principle that

   A. delegation of authority is more detailed at the top of the organizational structure
   B. detailed delegation of authority is associated with detailed work assignments
   C. delegation of authority should be in sufficient detail to prevent overlapping assignments
   D. detailed delegation of authority is associated with broad work assignments

9. In recent years, newer and more fluid types of organizational forms have been developed. One of these is a type of free-form organization.
Another name for this type of organization is the

   A. project organization
   B. semimix organization
   C. naturalistic structure
   D. semipermanent structure

10. Which of the following is the MAJOR objective of operational or management systems audits?

    A. Determining the number of personnel needed
    B. Recommending opportunities for improving operating and management practices
    C. Detecting fraud
    D. Determining organization problems

11. Assume that a manager observes that conflict exists between his agency and another operating agency of government.
Which of the following statements is the LEAST probable cause of this conflict?

    A. Incompatibility between the agencies' goals but similarity in their resource allocations
    B. Compatibility between agencies' goals and resources
    C. Status differences between agency personnel
    D. Differences in perceptions of each other's policies

12. Of the following, a MAJOR purpose of brainstorming as a problem-solving technique is to

    A. develop the ability to concentrate
    B. encourage creative thinking
    C. evaluate employees' ideas
    D. develop critical ability

13. The one of the following requirements which is LEAST likely to accompany regular delegation of work from a manager to a subordinate is a(n)

    A. need to review the organization's workload
    B. indication of what work the subordinate is to do
    C. need to grant authority to the subordinate
    D. obligation for the subordinate who accepts the work to try to complete it

14. Of the following, the one factor which is generally considered LEAST essential to successful committee operation is

    A. stating a clear definition of the authority and scope of the committee
    B. selecting the committee chairman carefully
    C. limiting the size of the committee to four persons
    D. limiting the subject matter to that which can be handled in group discussion

15. In using the program evaluation and review technique, the *critical path* is the path that

    A. requires the shortest time
    B. requires the longest time
    C. focuses most attention on social constraints
    D. focuses most attention on repetitious jobs

16. Which one of the following is LEAST characteristic of the management-by-objectives approach?

    A. The scope within which the employee may exercise decision-making is broadened
    B. The employee starts with a self-appraisal of his performances, abilities, and potential
    C. Emphasis is placed on activities performed; activities orientation is maximized
    D. Each employee participates in determining his own objectives

17. The function of management which puts into effect the decisions, plans, and programs that have previously been worked out for achieving the goals of the group is MOST appropriately called

    A. scheduling
    B. classifying
    C. budgeting
    D. directing

18. In the establishment of a plan to improve office productive efficiency, which of the following guidelines is LEAST helpful in setting sound work standards?

    A. Employees must accept the plan's objectives.
    B. Current production averages must be promulgated as work standards for a group.
    C. The work flow must generally be fairly constant.
    D. The operation of the plan must be expressed in terms understandable to the worker.

19. The one of the following activities which, generally speaking, is of *relatively* MAJOR importance at the lower-management level and of *somewhat* LESSER importance at higher-management levels is

    A. actuating
    B. forecasting
    C. organizing
    D. planning

20. Three styles of leadership exist: democratic, authoritarian, and laissez-faire. Of the following work situations, the one in which a democratic approach would normally be the MOST effective is when the work is

    A. routine and moderately complex
    B. repetitious and simple
    C. complex and not routine
    D. simple and not routine

21. Governmental and business organizations *generally* encounter the GREATEST difficulties in developing tangible measures of which one of the following?

    A. The level of expenditures
    B. Contributions to social welfare
    C. Retention rates
    D. Causes of labor unrest

22. Of the following, a *management-by-objectives* program is BEST described as

    A. a new comprehensive plan of organization
    B. introduction of budgets and financial controls
    C. introduction of long-range planning
    D. development of future goals with supporting and related progress reviews

23. Research and analysis is probably the most widely used technique for selecting alternatives when major planning decisions are involved.
    Of the following, a VALUABLE characteristic of research and analysis is that this technique

    A. places the problem in a meaningful conceptual framework
    B. involves practical application of the various alternatives
    C. accurately analyzes all important tangibles
    D. is much less expensive than other problem-solving methods

24. If a manager were assigned the task of using a systems approach to designing a new work unit, which of the following should he consider FIRST in carrying out his design?

    A. Networks
    B. Work flows and information processes
    C. Linkages and relationships
    D. Decision points and control loops

25. The MAIN distinction between Theory X and Theory Y approaches to organization, in accordance with Douglas McGregor's view, is that Theory Y

    A. considers that work is natural to people; Theory X assumes that people are lazy and avoid work
    B. leads to a tall, narrow organization structure, while Theory X leads to one that is flat
    C. organizations motivate people with money; Theory X organizations motivate people with good working conditions
    D. represents authoritarian management, while Theory X management is participative

KEY (CORRECT ANSWERS)

1. C
2. B
3. D
4. C
5. A

6. A
7. C
8. B
9. A
10. B

11. B
12. B
13. A
14. C
15. B

16. C
17. D
18. B
19. A
20. C

21. B
22. D
23. A
24. B
25. A

TEST 2

DIRECTIONS: Each question or incomplete statement is followed by several suggested answers or completions. Select the one that BEST answers the question or completes the statement. *PRINT THE LETTER OF THE CORRECT ANSWER IN THE SPACE AT THE RIGHT.*

1. Of the following, the stage in decision-making which is usually MOST difficult is

    A. stating the alternatives
    B. predicting the possible outcome of each alternative
    C. evaluating the relative merits of each alternative
    D. minimizing the undesirable aspects of the alternative selected

    1.____

2. In a department where a clerk is reporting both to a senior clerk in charge of the mail room and also to a supervising clerk in charge of the duplicating section, there may be a breakdown of the management principle called

    A. horizontal specialization   B. job enrichment
    C. unity of command   D. Graicunas' Law

    2.____

3. Of the following, the failure by line managers to accept and appreciate the benefits and limitations of a new program or system VERY frequently can be traced to the

    A. budgetary problems involved
    B. resultant need to reduce staff
    C. lack of controls it engenders
    D. failure of top management to support its implementation

    3.____

4. Although there is general agreement that *management by objectives* has made a major contribution to modern management of large organizations, criticisms of the system during the past few years have resulted in

    A. mounting pressure for relaxation of management goals
    B. renewed concern with human values and the manager's personal needs
    C. over-mechanistic application of the perceptions of the behavioral scientists
    D. disillusionment with *management by objectives* on the part of a majority of managers

    4.____

5. Of the following, which is usually considered to be a MAJOR obstacle to the systematic analysis of potential problems by managers?

    A. Managers have a tendency to think that all the implications of some proposed step cannot be fully understood.
    B. Rewards rarely go to those managers who are most successful at resolving current problems in management.
    C. There is a common conviction of managers that their goals are difficult to achieve.
    D. Managers are far more concerned about correcting today's problems than with preventing tomorrow's.

    5.____

6. Which of the following should generally have the MOST influence on the selection of supervisors?

    A. Experience within the work unit where the vacancies exist
    B. Amount of money needed to effect the promotion
    C. Personal preferences of the administration
    D. Evaluation of capacity to exercise supervisory responsibilities

7. In questioning a potential administrator for selection purposes, the one of the following practices which is MOST desirable is to

    A. encourage the job applicant to give primarily *yes* or *no* replies
    B. get the applicant to talk freely and in detail about his background
    C. let the job applicant speak most of the time
    D. probe the applicant's attitudes, motivation, and willingness to accept responsibility

8. In implementing the managerial function of training subordinates, it is USEFUL to know that a widely agreed-upon definition of human learning is that learning

    A. is a relatively permanent change in behavior that results from reinforced practice or experience
    B. involves an improvement, but not necessarily a change in behavior
    C. involves a change in behavior, but not necessarily an improvement
    D. is a temporary change in behavior which must be subject to practice or experience

9. If a manager were thinking about using a committee of subordinates to solve an operating problem, which of the following would generally NOT be an advantage of such use of the committee approach?

    A. Improved coordination   B. Low cost
    C. Increased motivation   D. Integrated judgment

10. Which one of the following management approaches MOST often uses model-building techniques to solve management problems?
    _____ approach

    A. Behavioral   B. Fiscal
    C. Quantitative   D. Process

11. Of the following, the MOST serious risk in using budgets as a tool for management control is the

    A. probable neglect of other good management practices
    B. likelihood of guesswork because of the need to plan far in advance
    C. possibility of undue emphasis on factors that are easiest to measure
    D. danger of making qualitative rather than quantitative assessments of performance

12. In government budgeting, the problem of relating financial transactions to the fiscal year in which they are budgeted is BEST met by

   A. determining the cash balance by comparing how much money has been received and how much has been paid out
   B. applying net revenue to the fiscal year in which they are collected as offset by relevant expenses
   C. adopting a system whereby appropriations are entered when they are received and expenditures are entered when they are paid out
   D. entering expenditures on the books when the obligation to make the expenditure is made

13. If the agency's bookkeeping system records income when it is received and expenditures when the money is paid out, this sytem is USUALLY known as a _____ system.

   A. cash
   B. flow-payment
   C. deferred
   D. fiscal year income

14. An audit, as the term applies to budget execution, is MOST NEARLY a

   A. procedure based on the budget estimates
   B. control exercised by the executive on the legislature in the establishment of program priorities
   C. check on the legality of expenditures and is based on the appropriations act
   D. requirement which must be met before funds can be spent

15. In government budgeting, there is a procedure known as *allotment*.
    Of the following statements which relate to allotment, select the one that is MOST generally considered to be correct.
    Allotment

   A. increases the practice of budget units coming back to the legislative branch for supplemental appropriations
   B. is simply an example of red tape
   C. eliminates the requirement of timing of expenditures
   D. is designed to prevent waste

16. In government budgeting, the establishment of the schedules of allotments is MOST generally the responsibility of the

   A. budget unit and the legislature
   B. budget unit and the executive
   C. budget unit *only*
   D. executive and the legislature

17. Of the following statements relating to preparation of an organization's budget request, which is the MOST generally valid precaution?

    A. Give specific instructions on the format of budget requests and required supporting data
    B. Because of the complexity of preparing a budget request, avoid argumentation to support the requests
    C. Put requests in whatever format is desirable
    D. Consider that final approval will be given to initial estimates

18. Of the following statements which relate to the budget process in a well-organized government, select the one that is MOST NEARLY correct.

    A. The budget cycle is the step-by-step process which is repeated each and every fiscal year.
    B. Securing approval of the budget does not take place within the budget cycle.
    C. The development of a new budget and putting it into effect is a two-step process known as the budget cycle.
    D. The fiscal period, usually a fiscal year, has no relation to the budget cycle.

19. If a manager were asked what PPBS stands for, he would be RIGHT if he said

    A. public planning budgeting system
    B. planning programming budgeting system
    C. planning projections budgeting system
    D. programming procedures budgeting system

Questions 20–21.

DIRECTIONS: Answer Questions 20 and 21 on the basis of the following information.

Sample Budget

Refuse Collection	Amount
Personal Services	$ 30,000
Contractual Services	5,000
Supplies and Materials	5,000
Capital Outlay	10,000
	$ 50,000

Residential Collections	
Dwellings–1 pickup per week	1,000
Tons of refuse collected per year	375
Cost of collections per ton	$ 8
Cost per dwelling pickup per year	$ 3
Total annual cost	$ 3,000

20. The sample budget shown is a simplified example of a _____ budget. 20.____

   A. factorial
   B. performance
   C. qualitative
   D. rational

21. The budget shown in the sample differs CHIEFLY from line-item and program budgets in that it includes 21.____

   A. objects of expenditure but not activities or functions
   B. only activities, functions, and control
   C. activities and functions but not objects of expenditures
   D. levels of service

Question 22.

DIRECTIONS: Answer Question 22 on the basis of the following information.

Sample Budget

Environmental Safety
   Air Pollution Protection
      Personal Services $20,000,000
      Contractual Services   4,000,000
      Supplies and Materials   4,000,000
      Capital Outlay   2,000,000
        Total Air Pollution Protection $ 30,000,000

   Water Pollution Protection
      Personal Services $23,000,000
      Supplies and Materials   4,500,000
      Capital Outlay   20,500,000
        Total Water Pollution Protection $ 48,000,000

   Total Environmental Safety $ 78,000,000

22. Based on the above budget, which is the MOST valid statement? 22.____

   A. Environmental Safety, Air Pollution Protection, and Water Pollution Protection could all be considered program elements.
   B. The object listings included water pollution protection and capital outlay.
   C. Examples of the program element listings in the above are personal services and supplies and materials.
   D. Contractual Services and Environmental Safety were the program element listings.

23. Which of the following is NOT an advantage of a program budget over a line-item budget? 23.____
    A program budget

   A. allows us to set up priority lists in deciding what activities we will spend our money on
   B. gives us more control over expenditures than a line-item budget
   C. is more informative in that we know the broad purposes of spending money
   D. enables us to see if one program is getting much less money than the others

24. If a manager were trying to explain the fundamental difference between traditional accounting theory and practice and the newer practice of managerial accounting, he would be MOST accurate if he said that

    A. traditional accounting practice focused on providing information for persons outside organizations, while managerial accounting focuses on providing information for people inside organizations
    B. traditional accounting practice focused on providing information for persons inside organizations while managerial accounting focuses on providing information for persons outside organizations
    C. managerial accounting is exclusively concerned with historical facts while traditional accounting stresses future projections exclusively
    D. traditional accounting practice is more budget-focused than managerial accounting

25. Which of the following formulas is used to determine the number of days required to process work?

    A. $\dfrac{\text{Employees} \times \text{Daily Output}}{\text{Volume}} = \text{Days to Process Work}$

    B. $\dfrac{\text{Volume} \times \text{Daily Output}}{\text{Employees}} = \text{Days to Process Work}$

    C. $\dfrac{\text{Volume}}{\text{Employees} \times \text{Daily Output}} = \text{Days to Process Work}$

    D. $\dfrac{\text{Employees} \times \text{Volume}}{\text{Daily Output}} = \text{Days to Process Work}$

KEY (CORRECT ANSWERS)

1. C
2. C
3. D
4. B
5. D

6. D
7. D
8. A
9. B
10. C

11. C
12. D
13. A
14. C
15. D

16. C
17. A
18. A
19. B
20. B

21. D
22. A
23. B
24. A
25. C

TEST 3

DIRECTIONS: Each question or incomplete statement is followed by several suggested answers or completions. Select the one that BEST answers the question or completes the statement. *PRINT THE LETTER OF THE CORRECT ANSWER IN THE SPACE AT THE RIGHT.*

1. Electronic data processing equipment can produce more information faster than can be generated by any other means.
   In view of this, the MOST important problem faced by management at present is to

   A. keep computers fully occupied
   B. find enough computer personnel
   C. assimilate and properly evaluate the information
   D. obtain funds to establish appropriate information systems

   1.____

2. A well-designed management information system ESSENTIALLY provides each executive and manager the information he needs for

   A. determining computer time requirements
   B. planning and measuring results
   C. drawing a new organization chart
   D. developing a new office layout

   2.____

3. It is generally agreed that management policies should be periodically reappraised and restated in accordance with current conditions.
   Of the following, the approach which would be MOST effective in determining whether a policy should be revised is to

   A. conduct interviews with staff members at all levels in order to ascertain the relationship between the policy and actual practice
   B. make proposed revisions in the policy and apply it to current problems
   C. make up hypothetical situations using both the old policy and a revised version in order to make comparisons
   D. call a meeting of top level staff in order to discuss ways of revising the policy

   3.____

4. Every manager has many occasions to lead a conference or participate in a conference of some sort.
   Of the following statements that pertain to conferences and conference leadership, which is generally considered to be MOST valid?

   A. Since World War II, the trend has been toward fewer shared decisions and more conferences.
   B. The most important part of a conference leader's job is to direct discussion.
   C. In providing opportunities for group interaction, management should avoid consideration of its past management philosophy.
   D. A good administrator cannot lead a good conference if he is a poor public speaker.

   4.____

5. Of the following, it is usually LEAST desirable for a conference leader to

   A. turn the question to the person who asked it
   B. summarize proceedings periodically
   C. make a practice of not repeating questions
   D. ask a question without indicating who is to reply

   5.____

6. The behavioral school of management thought bases its beliefs on certain assumptions. Which of the following is NOT a belief of this school of thought?

   A. People tend to seek and accept responsibility.
   B. Most people can be creative in solving problems.
   C. People prefer security above all else.
   D. Commitment is the most important factor in motivating people.

7. The one of the following objectives which would be LEAST appropriate as a major goal of research in the field of human resources management is to

   A. predict future conditions, events, and manpower needs
   B. evaluate established policies, programs, and practices
   C. evaluate proposed policies, programs, and practices
   D. identify deficient organizational units and apply suitable penalties

8. Of the following general interviewing methods or techniques, the one that is USUALLY considered to be effective in counseling, grievances, and appraisal interviews is the _____ interview.

   A. directed
   B. non-directed
   C. panel
   D. patterned

9. The ESSENTIAL first phase of decision-making is

   A. finding alternative solutions
   B. making a diagnosis of the problem
   C. selecting the plan to follow
   D. analyzing and comparing alternative solutions

10. Assume that, in a certain organization, a situation has developed in which there is little difference in status or authority between individuals.
    Which of the following would be the MOST likely result with regard to communication in this organization?

    A. Both the accuracy and flow of communication will be improved.
    B. Both the accuracy and flow of communication will substantially decrease.
    C. Employees will seek more formal lines of communication.
    D. Neither the flow nor the accuracy of communication will be improved over the former hierarchical structure.

11. The main function of many agency administrative offices is *information management*. Information that is received by an administrative officer may be classified as active or passive, depending upon whether or not it requires the recipient to take some action. Of the following, the item received which is clearly the MOST active information is

    A. an appointment of a new staff member
    B. a payment voucher for a new desk
    C. a press release concerning a past city event
    D. the minutes of a staff meeting

12. Which one of the following sets BEST describes the general order in which to teach an operation to a new employee?

    A. Prepare, present, tryout, follow-up
    B. Prepare, test, tryout, re-test
    C. Present, test, tryout, follow-up
    D. Test, present, follow-up, re-test

13. Of the following, public employees may be separated from public service

    A. for the same reasons which are generally acceptable for discharging employees in private industry
    B. only under the most trying circumstances
    C. under procedures that are neither formalized nor subject to review
    D. solely in extreme cases involving offenses of gravest character

14. Of the following, the one LEAST considered to be a communication barrier is

    A. group feedback
    B. charged words
    C. selective perception
    D. symbolic meanings

15. Of the following ways for a manager to handle his appointments, the BEST way, according to experts in administration, generally is to

    A. schedule his own appointments and inform his secretary not to reserve his time without his approval
    B. encourage everyone to make appointments through his secretary and tell her when he makes his own appointments
    C. see no one who has not made a previous appointment
    D. permit anyone to see him without an appointment

16. Assume that a manager decides to examine closely one of five units under his supervision to uncover problems common to all five.
    His research technique is MOST closely related to the method called

    A. experimentation
    B. simulation
    C. linear analysis
    D. sampling

17. If one views the process of management as a dynamic process, which one of the following functions is NOT a legitimate part of that process?

    A. Communication
    B. Decision-making
    C. Organizational slack
    D. Motivation

18. Which of the following would be the BEST statement of a budget-oriented purpose for a government administrator? To

    A. provide 200 hours of instruction in basic reading for 3500 adult illiterates at a cost of $1 million in the next fiscal year
    B. inform the public of adult educational programs
    C. facilitate the transfer to a city agency of certain functions of a federally-funded program which is being phased out
    D. improve the reading skills of the adult citizens in the city

19. Modern management philosophy and practices are changing to accommodate the expectations and motivations of organization personnel.
   Which of the following terms INCORRECTLY describes these newer managerial approaches?

   A. Rational management
   B. Participative management
   C. Decentralization
   D. Democratic supervision

20. Management studies support the hypothesis that, in spite of the tendency of employees to censor the information communicated to their supervisor, subordinates are MORE likely to communicate problem-oriented information upward when they have

   A. a long period of service in the organization
   B. a high degree of trust in the supervisor
   C. a high educational level
   D. low status on the organizational ladder

KEY (CORRECT ANSWERS)

1.	C	11.	A
2.	B	12.	A
3.	A	13.	A
4.	B	14.	A
5.	A	15.	B
6.	C	16.	D
7.	D	17.	C
8.	B	18.	A
9.	B	19.	A
10.	D	20.	B

EXAMINATION SECTION
TEST 1

DIRECTIONS: Each question or incomplete statement is followed by several suggested answers or completions. Select the one that BEST answers the question or completes the statement. *PRINT THE LETTER OF THE CORRECT ANSWER IN THE SPACE AT THE RIGHT.*

1. Which one of the following is LEAST likely to be an area or cause of trouble in the use of staff personnel?

    A. Misunderstanding of the role the staff personnel are supposed to play as a result of vagueness of definition of their duties and authority
    B. Tendency of staff personnel almost always to be older than line personnel at comparable salary levels with whom they must deal
    C. Selection of staff personnel who fail to have simultaneously both competence in their specialities and skill in staff work
    D. The staff person fails to understand mixed staff and operating duties

2. Which of the following is generally NOT a valid statement with respect to the supervisory process?

    A. General supervision is more effective than close supervision.
    B. Employee-centered supervisors lead more effectively than do production-centered supervisors.
    C. Employee satisfaction is directly related to productivity.
    D. Low-producing supervisors use techniques that are different from high-producing supervisors.

3. Which of the following is the MOST essential element for proper evaluation of the performance of subordinate supervisors?

    A. Careful definition of each supervisor's specific job responsibilities and of his progress in meeting mutually agreed upon work goals
    B. System of rewards and penalties based on each supervisor's progress in meeting clearly defined performance standards
    C. Definition of personality traits, such as industry, initiative, dependability, and cooperativeness, required for effective job performance
    D. Breakdown of each supervisor's job into separate components and a rating of his performance on each individual task

4. The PRINCIPAL advantage of specialization for the operating efficiency of a public service agency is that specialization

    A. reduces the amount of red tape in coordinating the activities of mutually dependent departments
    B. simplifies the problem of developing adequate job controls
    C. provides employees with a clear understanding of the relationship of their activities to the overall objectives of the agency
    D. reduces destructive competition for power between departments

5. A list of conditions which encourages good morale inside a work group would NOT include a

   A. high rate of agreement among group members on values and objectives
   B. tight control system to minimize the risk of individual error
   C. good possibility that joint action will accomplish goals
   D. past history of successful group accomplishment

6. Of the following, the MOST important factor to be considered in selecting a training strategy or program is the

   A. requirements of the job to be performed by the trainees
   B. educational level or prior training of the trainees
   C. size of the training group
   D. quality and competence of available training specialists

7. Of the following, the one which is considered to be LEAST characteristic of the higher ranks of management is

   A. that higher levels of management benefit from modern technology
   B. that success is measured by the extent to which objectives are achieved
   C. the number of subordinates that directly report to a manager
   D. the de-emphasis of individual and specialized performance

8. Assume that a manager is preparing a training syllabus to be used in training members of her staff.
   Which of the following would NOT be a valid principle of the learning process to consider when preparing this training syllabus?

   A. When a person has thoroughly learned a task, it takes a lot of effort to create a little more improvement.
   B. In complicated learning situations, there is a period in which an additional period of practice produces an equal amount of improvement in learning.
   C. The less a person knows about the task, the slower the initial progress.
   D. The more a person knows about the task, the slower the initial progress.

9. Which statement BEST illustrates when collective bargaining agreements are working well?

   A. Executives strongly support subordinate managers.
   B. The management rights clause in the contract is clear and enforced.
   C. Contract provisions are competently interpreted.
   D. The provisions of the agreement are properly interpreted, communicated, and observed.

10. An executive who wishes to encourage subordinates to communicate freely with him about a job-related problem should FIRST

    A. state his own position on the problem before listening to the subordinates' ideas
    B. invite subordinates to give their own opinions on the problem
    C. ask subordinates for their reactions to his own ideas about the problem
    D. guard the confidentiality of management information about the problem

11. The ability to deal constructively with intra-organizational conflict is an essential attribute of the successful manager.
    The one of the following types of conflict which would be LEAST difficult to handle constructively is a situation in which there is

    A. agreement on objectives, but disagreement as to the probable results of adopting the various alternatives
    B. agreement on objectives, disagreement on alternative courses of action, and relative certainty as to the outcome of one of the alternatives
    C. disagreement on objectives and on alternative courses of action, and relative certainty as to the outcome of one of the alternatives
    D. disagreement on objectives and on alternative courses of action, but uncertainty as to the outcome of the alternatives

12. Which of the following actions does NOT belong in a properly conducted grievance handling process?

    A. Gathering relevant information on why the grievance arose
    B. Formulating a personal judgment about the fairness or unfairness of the grievance at the time the grievance is presented
    C. Establishing tentative answers to the grievance
    D. Following up to see whether the solution has eliminated the difficulty

13. Grievances are generally defined as complaints expressed over work-related matters.
    Which one of the following is MOST important for managers to be aware of in connection with this definition?
    The

    A. fact that the definition fails to separate the subject of the grievance from the attitude of the grievant
    B. fact that anything in the organization may be the source of the grievance
    C. need to assume that dissatisfied people have adverse effects on productivity
    D. implication that management should be concerned about expressed grievances and unconcerned about unexpressed grievances

14. In carrying out disciplinary action, the MOST important procedure for all managers to follow is to

    A. convince all levels of management on the need for discipline from the organization's viewpoint
    B. follow up on a disciplinary action and not assume that the action has been effective
    C. convince all executives that proper discipline is a legitimate tool for their use
    D. convince all executives that they need to display confidence in the organization's rules

15. Assume that an employee under your supervision is acquitted in court of criminal charges arising out of his employment.
    Of the following statements concerning disciplinary action, which is MOST NEARLY correct?

    A. Disciplinary proceedings against the employee may not be held for the same offenses on which he was tried and acquitted.
    B. In a disciplinary action, the acquittal dispenses with the requirement that the employee be advised as to his constitutional rights.
    C. Civil Rights Law Section 79 prohibits the taking of any further punitive action by an employer if the offense did not involve official corruption.
    D. It is possible for the employee to be found guilty of the same offense when tried in a departmental hearing.

16. Work rules can be an effective tool in the process of personnel management.
    The BEST practical definition for work rules is that they are

    A. minimum standards of conduct or performance that apply to individuals or groups at work in an organization
    B. prescriptions that serve to specialize employee behavior
    C. predetermined decisions about disciplinary action
    D. the major determinant of an organization's climate and the morale of its workforce

Questions 17-18

DIRECTIONS: Questions 17 and 18 pertain to identification of words that are incorrectly used because they are not in keeping with the meaning of the quotation. In answering each question, the first step is to read the passage and identify the incorrectly used word, and then select the word which, when substituted, BEST serves to convey the meaning of the quotation.

17. Among the Housing Manager's overall responsibilities in administering a project is the prevention of the development of conditions which might lead to termination of tenancy and eviction of a tenant. Where there appears to be doubt that a tenant is fully aware of his responsibilities and is thus jeopardizing his tenancy, the Housing Manager should acquaint him with these responsibilities. Where a situation involves behavior of a tenant or a member of his family, the Housing Manager should confirm, through discussions and referrals to social agencies, correction of the conditions before they reach a state where there is no alternative but termination proceedings.

   A. Coordinate
   B. Identify
   C. Assert
   D. Attempt

18. The one universal administrative complaint is that the budget is inadequate. Between adequacy and inadequacy lie all degrees of adequacy. Further, human wants are modest in relation to human resources. From these two facts we may conclude that the fundamental criterion of administrative decision must be a criterion of efficiency (the degree to which the goals have been reached relative to the available resources) rather than a criterion of adequacy (the degree to which its goals have been reached). The task of the manager is to maximize social values relative to limited resources.

   A. Improve
   B. Simple
   C. Limitless
   D. Optimize

Questions 19-21.

DIRECTIONS: Questions 19 through 21 are to be answered SOLELY on the basis of the following situation.

John Foley, a top administrator, is responsible for output in his organization. Because productivity had been lagging for two periods in a row, Foley decided to establish a committee of his subordinate managers to investigate the reasons for the poor performance and to make recommendations for improvements. After two meetings, the committee came to the conclusions and made the recommendations that follow.

Output forecasts had been handed down from the top without prior consultation with middle management and first level supervision. Lines of authority and responsibility had been unclear. The planning and control process should be decentralized.

After receiving the committee's recommendations, Foley proceeded to take the following actions. Foley decided he would retain final authority to establish quotas but would delegate to the middle managers the responsibility for meeting quotas.

After receiving Foley's decision, the middle managers proceeded to delegate to the first-line supervisors the authority to establish their own quotas. The middle managers eventually received and combined the first-line supervisors' quotas so that these conformed to Foley's.

19. Foley's decision to delegate responsibility for meeting quotas to the middle managers is inconsistent with sound management principles because

    A. Foley should not have involved himself in the first place
    B. middle managers do not have the necessary skills
    C. quotas should be established by the chief executive
    D. responsibility should not be delegated

20. The principle of co-extensiveness of responsibility and authority bears on Foley's decision.
    In this case, it implies that

    A. authority should exceed responsibility
    B. authority should be delegated to match the degree of responsibility
    C. both authority and responsibility should be retained and not delegated
    D. responsibility should be delegated, but authority should be retained

21. The middle managers' decision to delegate to the first-line supervisors the authority to establish quotas was INCORRECTLY reasoned because

    A. delegation and control must go together
    B. first-line supervisors are in no position to establish quotas
    C. one cannot delegate authority that one does not possess
    D. the meeting of quotas should not be delegated

22. If one attempts to list the advantages of the management-by-exception principle as it is used in connection with the budgeting process, several distinct advantages could be cited.
    Which of the following is NOT an advantage of this principle as it applies to the budgeting process?
    Management-by-exception

    A. saves time
    B. identifies critical problem areas
    C. focuses attention and concentrates effort
    D. escalates the frequency and importance of budget-related decisions

23. The MOST accurate description of a budget is that

    A. a budget is made up by an organization to plan its future activities
    B. a budget specifies in dollars and cents how much is spent in a particular time period
    C. a budget specifies how much the organization to which it relates estimates it will spend over a certain period of time
    D. all plans dealing with money are budgets

24. Of the following, the one which is NOT a contribution that a budget makes to organizational programming is that a budget

    A. enables a comparison of what actually happened with what was expected
    B. stresses the need to forecast specific goals and eliminates the need to focus on tasks needed to accomplish goals
    C. may illustrate duplication of effort between interdependent activities
    D. shows the relationship between various organizational segments

25. A line-item budget is a good control budget because

    A. it clearly specifies how the items being purchased will be used
    B. expenditures can be shown primarily for contractual services
    C. it clearly specifies what the money is buying
    D. it clearly specifies the services to be provided

KEY (CORRECT ANSWERS)

1.	B	11.	B
2.	C	12.	B
3.	A	13.	C
4.	B	14.	B
5.	B	15.	D
6.	A	16.	A
7.	A	17.	D
8.	D	18.	C
9.	D	19.	D
10.	B	20.	B

21.	C
22.	D
23.	C
24.	B
25.	C

TEST 2

DIRECTIONS: Each question or incomplete statement is followed by several suggested answers or completions. Select the one that BEST answers the question or completes the statement. *PRINT THE LETTER OF THE CORRECT ANSWER IN THE SPACE AT THE RIGHT.*

1. The insights of Chester I. Barnard have influenced the development of management thought in significant ways. He is MOST closely identified with a position that has become known as the

   A. acceptance theory of authority
   B. principle of the manager's or executive's span of control
   C. *Theory X* and *Theory Y* dichotomy
   D. unit of command principle

2. Certain conditions should exist to insure that a subordinate will decide to accept a communication as being authoritative.
   Which of the following is LEAST valid as a condition which should exist?

   A. The subordinate understands the communication.
   B. At the time of the subordinate's decision, he views the communication as consistent with the organization's purpose and his personal interest.
   C. At the time of the subordinate's decision, he views the communication as more consistent with his personal purposes than with the organization's interest.
   D. The subordinate is mentally and physically able to comply with the communication.

3. In exploring the effects that employee participation has on implementing changes in work methods, certain relationships have been established between participation and productivity.
   It has MOST generally been found that highest productivity occurs in groups provided with

   A. participation in the process of change only through representatives of their group
   B. no participation in the change process
   C. full participation in the change process
   D. intermittent participation in the process of change

4. The trend LEAST likely to occur in the area of employee-management relations is that

   A. employees will exert more influence on decisions affecting their interests
   B. technological change will have a stronger impact on organizations' human resources
   C. labor will judge management according to company profits
   D. government will play a larger role in balancing the interests of the parties in labor-management affairs

5. Members of an organization must satisfy several fundamental psychological needs in order to be happy and productive.
   The BROADEST and MOST basic needs are

   A. achievement, recognition, and acceptance
   B. competition, recognition, and accomplishment
   C. salary increments and recognition
   D. acceptance of competition and economic award

6. Morale has been defined as the capacity of a group of people to pull together steadily for a common purpose.
   Morale thus defined is MOST generally dependent on

   A. job security
   B. group and individual self-confidence
   C. organizational efficiency
   D. physical health of the individuals

7. Which is the CORRECT order of steps to follow when revising office procedure?
   To

   I. develop the improved method as determined by time and motion studies and effective workplace layout
   II. find out how the task is now performed
   III. apply the new method
   IV. analyze the current method

   The CORRECT answer is:
   A. IV, II, I, III
   B. II, I, III, IV
   C. I, II, IV, III
   D. II, IV, I, III

8. In contrast to broad spans of control, narrow spans of control are MOST likely to

   A. provide opportunity for more personal contact between superior and subordinate
   B. encourage decentralization
   C. stress individual initiative
   D. foster group of team effort

9. A manager is coaching a subordinate on the nature of decision-making. She could BEST define decision-making as

   A. choosing between alternatives
   B. making diagnoses of feasible ends
   C. making diagnoses of feasible means
   D. comparing alternatives

10. Of the following, the LEAST valid purpose of an organizational policy statement is to

    A. keep personnel from performing improper actions and functions on routine matters
    B. prevent the mishandling of non-routine matters
    C. provide management personnel with a tool that precludes the need for their use of judgment
    D. provide standard decisions and approaches in handling problems of a recurrent nature

11. Current thinking on bureaucratic organizations is that

    A. bureaucracy is on the way out
    B. bureaucracy, though not perfect, is unlikely to be replaced
    C. bureaucratic organizations are most effective in dealing with constant change
    D. bureaucratic organizations are most effective when dealing with sophisticated customers or clients

12. The development of alternate plans as a major step in planning will normally result in the planner's having several possible course of action available. GENERALLY, this is

    A. *desirable* since such development helps to determine the most suitable alternative and to provide for the unexpected
    B. *desirable* since such development makes the use of planning premises and constraints unnecessary
    C. *undesirable* since the planners should formulate only one way of achieving given goals at a given time
    D. *undesirable* since such action restricts efforts to modify the planning to take advantage of opportunities

13. Assume a manager carries out his responsibilities to his staff according to what is now known about managerial leadership.
    Which of the following statements would MOST accurately reflect his assumptions about proper management?

    A. Efficiency in operations results from allowing the human element to participate in a minimal way.
    B. Efficient operation results from balancing work considerations with personnel considerations.
    C. Efficient operation results from a work force committed to its self-interest.
    D. Efficient operation results from staff relationships that produce a friendly work climate.

14. Assume that a manager is called upon to conduct a management audit. To do this properly, he would have to take certain steps in a specific sequence. Which step should this manager take FIRST?

    A. Managerial performance must be surveyed.
    B. A method of reporting must be established.
    C. Management auditing procedures and documentation must be developed.
    D. Criteria for the audit must be established.

15. If a manager is required to conduct a scientific investigation of an organizational problem, the FIRST step he should take is to

    A. state his assumptions about the problem
    B. carry out a search for background information
    C. choose the right approach to investigate the validity of his assumptions
    D. define and state the problem

16. A manager would be correct to assert that the principle of delegation states that decisions should be made PRIMARILY

    A. by persons in an executive capacity qualified to make them
    B. by persons in a non-executive capacity
    C. at as low an organizational level of authority as practicable
    D. by the next lower level of authority

17. Of the following, which one is NOT regarded by management authorities as a fundamental characteristic of an ideal bureaucracy?

    A. Division of labor and specialization
    B. An established hierarchy
    C. Decentralization of authority
    D. A set of operating rules and regulations

18. As the number of subordinates in a manager's span of control increases, the actual number of possible relationships

    A. increases disproportionately to the number of subordinates
    B. increases in equal number to the number of subordinates
    C. reaches a stable level
    D. will first increase, then slowly decrease

19. Management experts generally believe that computer-based management information systems (MIS) have greater potential for improving the process of management than any other development in recent decades.
The one of the following which MOST accurately describes the objectives of MIS is to

   A. provide information for decision-making on planning, initiating, and controlling the operations of the various units of the organization
   B. establish mechanization of routine functions such as clerical records, payroll, inventory, and accounts receivable in order to promote economy and efficiency
   C. computerize decision-making on planning, initiating, organizing, and controlling the operations of an organization
   D. provide accurate facts and figures on the various programs of the organization to be used for purposes of planning and research

20. The one of the following which is the BEST application of the *management-by-exception* principle is that this principle

   A. stimulates communication and aids in management of crisis situations, thus reducing the frequency of decision-making
   B. saves time and reserves top management decisions only for crisis situations, thus reducing the frequency of decision-making
   C. stimulates communication, saves time, and reduces the frequency of decision-making
   D. is limited to crisis-management situations

21. Generally, each organization is dependent upon the availability of qualified personnel.
Of the following, the MOST important factor affecting the availability of qualified people to each organization is

   A. availability of public transportation
   B. the general rise in the educational levels of our population
   C. the rise of sentiment against racial discrimination
   D. pressure by organized community groups

22. A fundamental responsibility of all managers is to decide what physical facilities and equipment are needed to help attain basic goals.
Good planning for the purchase and use of equipment is seldom easy to do and is complicated most by the fact that

   A. organizations rarely have stable sources of supply
   B. nearly all managers tend to be better at personnel planning than at equipment planning
   C. decisions concerning physical resources are made too often on an emergency basis rather than under carefully prepared policies
   D. legal rulings relative to depreciation fluctuate very frequently

23. In attempting to reconcile managerial objectives and an individual employee's goals, it is generally LEAST desirable for management to

   A. recognize the capacity of the individual to contribute toward realization of managerial goals
   B. encourage self-development of the employee to exceed minimum job performance
   C. consider an individual employee's work separately from other employees
   D. demonstrate that an employee advances only to the extent that he contributes directly to the accomplishment of stated goals

24. As a management tool for discovering individual training needs, a job analysis would generally be of LEAST assistance in determining

   A. the performance requirements of individual jobs
   B. actual employee performance on the job
   C. acceptable standards of performance
   D. training needs for individual jobs

25. One of the major concerns of organizational managers today is how the spread of automation will affect them and the status of their positions. Realistically speaking, one can say that the MOST likely effect of our newer forms of highly automated technology on managers will be to

   A. make most top-level positions superfluous or obsolete
   B. reduce the importance of managerial work in general
   C. replace the work of managers with the work of technicians
   D. increase the importance of and demand for top managerial personnel

KEY (CORRECT ANSWERS)

1.	A	11.	B
2.	C	12.	A
3.	C	13.	B
4.	C	14.	D
5.	A	15.	D
6.	B	16.	C
7.	D	17.	C
8.	A	18.	A
9.	A	19.	A
10.	C	20.	C

21. B
22. C
23. C
24. B
25. D

EXAMINATION SECTION
TEST 1

DIRECTIONS: Each question or incomplete statement is followed by several suggested answers or completions. Select the one that BEST answers the question or completes the statement. *PRINT THE LETTER OF THE CORRECT ANSWER IN THE SPACE AT THE RIGHT.*

1. Several employees complain informally to their supervisor regarding some new procedures which have been instituted. The supervisor should immediately

    A. explain that management is responsible
    B. investigate the complaint
    C. refer the matter to the methods analyst
    D. tell the employees to submit their complaint as a formal grievance

    1.____

2. The PRINCIPAL aim of an administrator is to

    A. act as liaison between employee and management
    B. get the work done
    C. keep up morale
    D. train his subordinates

    2.____

3. Work measurement can be applied to operations where workload can be related to

    A. available personnel for the implementation of assigned tasks
    B. follow-up programs for continued progress
    C. cost abatement and optimum efficiency
    D. man hour utilization on assigned tasks

    3.____

4. The one of the following which is NOT a primary advantage of a work measurement program is

    A. the selection of informed personnel
    B. knowledge of personnel needs
    C. support of personnel requests
    D. setting of approximate unit costs

    4.____

5. A program of work measurement would be LEAST likely to

    A. point up the need for management research
    B. keep workload and personnel on an even keel
    C. measure the performance in exceptional operations
    D. evaluate the status of operations

    5.____

6. *Generally speaking, there are two kinds of work measurement:*
    (1) the traditional industrial engineering kind where performance standards are determined by time study or other engineering techniques, and (2) the statistical kind where yardsticks (so-called to distinguish them from engineered standards) are developed from a statistical analysis of past performance data. These data consist essentially of periodic reports in which work performed, expressed in identifiable work units, is related to the time required to perform it, usually expressed in man-hours.
    The ESSENTIAL difference between the two kinds of work measurement is that

    6.____

A. the statistical type is based on past, current, and future determinants of a diversent nature, while engineered standards are restrictive
B. yardsticks are less restrictive than engineered standards
C. time study standards employ a higher ratio of manhour data than do statistical standards
D. engineered standards are more costly as well as more accurate than routine time study methods

7. Government has favored the use of the statistical type of work measurement over the industrial type MAINLY because

   A. government is an institution rarely hampered by money seeking techniques
   B. as the statistical type of work measurement is broadly based, it is more capable of filling the wide expanse of government's needs
   C. employees might object vehemently against speed-ups, thereby sapping work measurement's force
   D. the former appears to be just as effective and less expensive than the latter

8. A work measurement program is a system by which a

   A. periodic account is kept of individual and group performance
   B. recurring account is kept of group performance
   C. periodic account is kept of performance by an individual
   D. periodic account is kept of performance by a group

9. Statistical standards developed during the early stages of a work measurement program are

   A. changed too rapidly and thus are of little value in the final program
   B. subject to change as the program moves forward
   C. incorporated into the final program, ultimately for research studies
   D. abandoned before the effective date of the final program

10. It is NOT an objective of a work measurement program to

    A. furnish a basis for procedural control
    B. provide a true basis for management control
    C. furnish a genuine basis for budget control
    D. provide a basis for management planning

11. The MOST valid of the following concepts of management control is that it examines

    A. the method with which work assignments have been accomplished in accordance with preconceived plans and policies
    B. preconceived plans and policies to determine their ultimate value
    C. results to determine how well work assignments have been accomplished in accordance with preconceived plans and policies
    D. the work of individual employees to get an acceptable standard, so as not to endanger the entire control program

12. Of the following, the LEAST likely area in which a deficiency in operations would be revealed by a work measurement program is

    A. improper personnel utilization
    B. inadequate equipment
    C. distribution of work
    D. personnel rating

13. The MOST accurate of the following statements regarding the standard as used in a work measurement program is:

    A. standard rates of performance should not be established until the effectiveness of an operation has been determined
    B. the measure of effectiveness should be kept separate and distinct from the application of standards to actual performance
    C. standards should not be used as guides in planning
    D. standard rates of performance must be established before effectiveness of an operation can be determined

14. The first and most important basic consideration in instituting a program of work measurement is the

    A. indoctrination of personnel
    B. establishment of a uniform technology
    C. selection of the time unit
    D. selection of a standard

15. A _____ is an item or a group of items, generally physical, which, when taken in the aggregate, serve to measure amounts of work.

    A. Therblig   B. function
    C. operation   D. work unit

16. Which of the following epitomizes the *raison d'etre* of work simplification?

    A. Waste elimination   B. Empirical costs
    C. Time study speed-ups   D. Charting techniques

17. A process charting analysis is likely to be of little value in the event of

    A. a major change in the department's activity
    B. a new supervisor from the outside coming in to head the unit
    C. increase in volume of work
    D. sizable personnel turnover

18. Staff or functional supervision in an organization

    A. is least justified at the operational level
    B. is contrary to the principle of Unity of Command
    C. is more effective than authoritative supervision
    D. normally does not give the right to take direct disciplinary action

19. The correlation between a flow process chart and a flow diagram is BEST described by which of the following statements?

   A. A flow process chart is supportive machinery to the flow diagram.
   B. In essence, the flow process chart exhibits time, distance, and location using standard symbols, whereas the flow diagram exhibits flow lines and uses classificational symbols.
   C. Much of the information on the flow process chart is reproduced from the flow diagram.
   D. The flow diagram is complementary to the flow process chart.

20. Indicate which statement is LEAST apt to clarify the underlying distinction between work simplification and other methods of betterment procedures.
   Work simplification

   A. is dependent on supervisory participation
   B. is designed for employee participation
   C. emphasizes group participation
   D. emphasizes the ideas of experts

21. In describing the process of administrative management, the LEAST valid description is that it

   A. is composed of interdependent functions
   B. is comprised of related parts
   C. is cyclical
   D. consists of independent parts

22. Work activity, as to type, individual performance, and time expenditure, is BEST illustrated by a _____ chart.

   A. flow process   B. work flow
   C. work distribution   D. operations

23. Neither the work distribution nor the flow process chart furnishes adequate intelligence as to

   A. methods   B. activities
   C. nature of work activity   D. unit prices

24. A graphic presentation of the steps and distribution through which each copy of a multiple copy office form travels is a(n)

   A. work distribution chart   B. flow process chart
   C. flow diagram   D. operations chart

25. A CHIEF target of work simplification is

   A. the achievement of greater productivity with the same work effort
   B. obtaining the same work accomplishment with less effort
   C. employee participation and little resistance to change
   D. all of the above

KEY (CORRECT ANSWERS)

1. B
2. B
3. D
4. A
5. C

6. B
7. D
8. B
9. B
10. A

11. C
12. D
13. D
14. B
15. D

16. A
17. B
18. D
19. D
20. D

21. D
22. C
23. D
24. C
25. C

TEST 2

DIRECTIONS: Each question or incomplete statement is followed by several suggested answers or completions. Select the one that BEST answers the question or completes the statement. *PRINT THE LETTER OF THE CORRECT ANSWER IN THE SPACE AT THE RIGHT.*

1. In conducting a work simplification program, which of the following office problems is the MOST likely to be solved by the use of the flow process chart?

    A. Are the employees deluged with unrelated tasks?
    B. What activities are the most costly, in terms of time consumed?
    C. Is the proper sequence of work activity employed?
    D. Is there an even distribution of work among the employees?

2. In the matter of procedural analysis, which question should be asked FIRST?

    A. When should the step be performed?
    B. Who should perform the step?
    C. What is the significance of the step?
    D. Where can this be improved upon?

3. Storage on a movement diagram is represented by

    A. ◇
    B. ▽
    C. ▢
    D. none of the above

4. The use of a flow process chart is LEAST desirable in indicating

    A. the time rate for each step
    B. distance travelled
    C. equipment-facilities layout
    D. sequence of activities

5. Division of work is BEST delineated by means of a _____ chart.

    A. work methods
    B. flow process
    C. work distribution
    D. flow authority

6. In seeking to conduct a work simplification analysis, the MOST appropriate first step would be to

    A. chart the procedures
    B. survey the facilities as to spatial access
    C. make problem area determination
    D. set up composition of forms analysis

7. The conception of a standard is BEST denoted as a

    A. hypothetical level
    B. circumscribed level of work activity
    C. level of comparing
    D. quintessential ideal

8. With reference to office work simplification, it could be considered expedient to

   A. first simplify the procedure and then the individual methods
   B. simplify the individual methods first, then the procedure
   C. concurrently, simplify the methods and the procedure
   D. none of the above

9. The MOST valid precept relative to work analysis is

   A. the volume of work is inversely proportional to the distribution or sequence of work
   B. in meeting production standards, the sequence of work transcends its distribution
   C. work sequence and work distribution should be analyzed in relation to work volume
   D. work sequence and work distribution should be examined for work validation concepts

10. The flow process chart is PRINCIPALLY used

    A. as a useful tool to train new employees
    B. to ascertain the effectiveness of the organization's employees
    C. to pinpoint *bottlenecks* affecting an operation
    D. to determine the visibility of organizational relationships

11. The work distribution chart would generally be of little value in answering which of the following questions?

    A. In what order are the activities being carried out?
    B. Which activities consume the most time?
    C. Is a work balance maintained among the employees?
    D. Are the employees laboring under a plethora of unrelated tasks?

12. A worthwhile analytical tool in work simplification is the flow process chart.
    The MOST valid description is that

    A. a flow process chart is generally reliable without review for a period of a year
    B. the flow process chart should be reviewed and possibly revised at six-month intervals
    C. the flow process chart is an ad hoc instrument
    D. the value of a flow process chart is not determined by time

13. In the analysis of a method of procedure in a work simplification program, a competent analyst should FIRST focalize on the clearance or diminution of

    A. verifications   B. transportations
    C. inspections   D. storages

14. Which one of the following statements BEST distinguishes a method from a procedure?

    A. A method is a consistent sequence of procedures.
    B. A procedure comprises a sequence of related methods, performed in most instances by a single person.
    C. A series of related methods comprise a procedure.
    D. In breadth, a method takes precedence over a procedure.

15. The data provided by the flow process chart in a work simplification program is INADEQUATE to answer which one of the following questions?

    A. What is being performed?
    B. In what manner should the work be performed?
    C. What is the quantity of work performed?
    D. Who should perform the work?

Questions 16-17.

DIRECTIONS: Questions 16 and 17 are to be answered on the basis of the following passage.

Ideally, then, the process of budget formulation would consist of a flow of directives down the organization, and a reverse flow of recommendations in terms of alternatives among which selection would be made at every level. Ideally, also, a change in the recommendations at any level would require reconsideration and revision at all lower levels. By a process of successive approximation, everything would be taken into account and all points of view harmonized. Such a process, however, would be ideal only if the future could be foreseen clearly and time did not matter. As it is, in a complicated organization like the Federal government, the initial policy objectives established for the budget become out-of-date, before such a procedure could be carried through. While this difficulty does not in any way impugn the principle that the budget should be considered in terms of alternatives, it may call for short-cut methods of estimation rather than long drawn-out ones.

16. According to the above passage,

    A. the ideal method for estimating purposes is a short one
    B. the ideal method is not ideal for use in the Federal government
    C. directives should flow up and down via short methods
    D. the Federal government needs to speed up its reverse flow of recommendations for greater budgetary estimates

17. A suitable title for the above passage would be

    A. FORMULATING THE FEDERAL GOVERNMENT'S BUDGETARY PRINCIPLES
    B. DIRECTIVES AND RECOMMENDATIONS: BUDGETARY FLOW
    C. THE PROCESS OF BUDGET FORMULATION
    D. THE APPLICATION OF THE IDEAL ESTIMATE TO THE FEDERAL GOVERNMENT

Questions 18-19.

DIRECTIONS: Questions 18 and 19 are to be answered in accordance with the following passage.

For purposes of budget formulation, the association of budgeting with accounting is less fortunate. Preparing for the future and recording the past do not necessarily require the same aptitudes or attitudes. The task of the accountant is to record past transactions in meticulous detail. Budgeting involves estimates of an uncertain future. But, because of the influence of accounts, government's budgets are prepared in a degree of detail that is quite unwarranted by the uncertain assumptions on which the estimates are based. A major source of government waste could be eliminated if estimates were prepared in no greater detail than was justified by their accuracy.

18. The author of the above paragraph

    A. is undermining the accounting profession
    B. believes accountants dwell solely in the past and cannot deal with the future efficiently
    C. wants the accountants out of government unless they become more accurate in their findings
    D. wishes to redirect the accountants' handling of budget procedures

19. The author's attitude appears to be

    A. tongue-in-cheek   B. morose
    C. strident   D. constructive

20. The idea that classic organizational structure tends to create work situations having requirements counter to those for psychological success and self-esteem, sometimes called the *organizational dilemma*, is MOST closely associated with

    A. Argyris   B. Taylor   C. Gulick   D. Maslow

Questions 21-25.

DIRECTIONS: Questions 21 through 25 contain incorrectly used words which change the meaning of the statement. Identify the word in the statement that is incorrect and select the choice that would make the sentence correct.

21. Standards of production performance are necessary to reveal the quantities of material, the number of hours of labor, the machine hours, and quantities of service (as, for example, power, steam, etc.) necessary to perform the various production operations. The establishment of such standards is an engineering rather than an accounting task, but it should be emphasized that such standards are needless to the development of the budgetary procedure—at least insofar as the budget is to serve as a tool of control. Such standards serve not only in the development of the budget and in measuring efficiency of production performance, but also in developing purchase requirements and in estimating costs.

    A. Manifest   B. Evaluation
    C. Essential   D. Function

22. Where standard costs are not available or their use is impracticable due to uncertainty of prices, estimates of the costs must be made on the basis of past experience and expected conditions. Ability to use standards largely eliminates the use of the budget for purposes of control of costs but its value remains for purposes of coordination of the program with purchases and finance.

    A. Failure   B. Current
    C. Culmination   D. Apparent

23. While one of the first objectives of the labor budget is to provide the highest practicable degree of regularity of employment, consideration must also be given to the estimating and perdurability of labor cost. Regularity of employment in itself effects some reduction in labor cost, but when carried beyond the point of practicability, it may increase other costs. For example, additional sales effort may be required to expand sales volume or to develop new products for slack periods; the cost of carrying inventories and the dangers of obsolescence and price declines must also be considered. A proper balance must be secured.

    A. Material   B. Control   C. Futures   D. To

24. The essentials of budgeting perhaps can be summarized in this manner:
    1. Develop a sound business program.
    2. Report on the progress in achieving that program.
    3. Take necessary action as to all variances which are inevitable.
    4. Revise the program to meet the changing conditions as required.

    A. Perfect   B. Plans
    C. Controllable   D. Secure

25. If a planning and control procedure is considered worthwhile, then it is a syllogism that preparation for the installation should be adequate. Time devoted to this educational aspect ordinarily will prove quite rewarding. The management to be involved with the budget, and particularly the middle management, must have a clear understanding of the budgetary procedure.

    A. Acquired   B. Remedial
    C. Monetary   D. Truism

KEY (CORRECT ANSWERS)

1.	D	11.	A
2.	C	12.	D
3.	D	13.	D
4.	C	14.	C
5.	C	15.	C
6.	C	16.	B
7.	C	17.	C
8.	A	18.	D
9.	C	19.	D
10.	C	20.	A

21. C
22. B
23. B
24. C
25. D

TEST 3

DIRECTIONS: Each question or incomplete statement is followed by several suggested answers or completions. Select the one that BEST answers the question or completes the statement. *PRINT THE LETTER OF THE CORRECT ANSWER IN THE SPACE AT THE RIGHT.*

1. The MOST important element in job satisfaction is   1.____

    A. job security
    B. responsibility or recognition
    C. salary
    D. type of supervision

2. The point of view that the average person wishes to avoid responsibility, wishes to be directed, has little ambition, and wants security above all, is described by Douglas MacGregor as Theory   2.____

    A. X
    C. Z
    B. Y
    D. X and Y combined

3. To prepare a work distribution chart, two other types of lists must generally be prepared. In usual order of preparation, they are a(n) _____ and a(n) _____ list.   3.____

    A. flow chart; activity
    B. skills list; task
    C. task list; activity
    D. activity list; task

4. A statistical control program in an office is valuable to detect deterioration in operations. It is, however, LEAST likely to reveal   4.____

    A. when preventative action is needed
    B. when a variation is due to chance
    C. when an assignable cause is present
    D. what the cause of error or deterioration is

5. Which of the following BEST defines an organization chart? An organizational chart   5.____

    A. depicts informal channels of communication within an organization
    B. depicts the major functions of an organization and the normal work flow between subdivisions of the organization
    C. presents graphically the arrangement and interrelationships of the subdivisions and the functions of the organization as they exist
    D. presents graphically the arrangement and relationships of all the positions authorized in an organization

6. In considering an office layout for a unit, which of the following factors should generally receive the LEAST consideration?   6.____

    A. Lighting levels in the existing area
    B. Major work flow—the processing of paper
    C. Present and projected growth rate of the unit
    D. Traffic patterns of employees and visitors

7. The BEST way to secure effective management is usually to

   A. allow staff to help solve administrative problems of line management
   B. provide a good organization structure
   C. select capable managers
   D. set up conservative spans of control

8. Which of the following is NOT an advantage of oral instructions as compared with written instructions?
   Oral

   A. instructions can be easily changed
   B. instructions are superior in transmitting complex directives
   C. instructions facilitate exchange of information between a superior and his subordinate(s)
   D. discussions are possible with oral instructions, making it easier to ascertain understanding

9. Which organization principle is MOST closely related to procedural analysis and improvement?

   A. Duplication, overlapping, and conflict should be eliminated.
   B. The objectives of the organization should be clearly defined.
   C. Managerial authority should be clearly defined.
   D. Top management should be freed of burdensome details.

10. Of the following control techniques, a _____ is MOST useful on large, complex projects.

    A. general work plan   B. Gantt chart
    C. monthly progress report   D. PERT chart

11. Work is organized so that the work is broken down into a series of jobs. Each unit of work moves progressively from position to position until completion.
    This paragraph BEST describes a

    A. parallel plan of work subdivision
    B. serial plan
    C. unit assembly plan
    D. unit process plan

12. According to the classic studies of Rensis Likert, the GREATEST factor making for good morale and increased productivity was having a

    A. good program of employee benefits and wage scales
    B. supervisor who gave his employees free rein after they were fully trained and did not interfere with them
    C. supervisor who was primarily interested in production
    D. supervisor who, while interested in production, was primarily *employee-centered*

13. The managerial grid shows two concerns and a range of interaction between them. In this grid, the horizontal axis indicates a concern for _____ and the vertical axis indicates a concern for _____.

    A. production; people   B. hierarchy; people
    C. organization; people   D. people; costs

14. It has been decided to make a few important revisions in the methods and procedures of a particular work unit. Of the following, which method of implementing these revisions would probably be the MOST desirable in terms of morale and of efficiency?

   A. Give all employees in unit individual instructions in the revised procedures and make sure each employee knows them before instructing the next.
   B. Institute all revisions at once followed by on-the-job training for all members of the work unit.
   C. Introduce the revisions one at a time and accompany each revision with an orientation for employees.
   D. Set up a training course for the employees which instructs them in all aspects of the revised procedures prior to their implementation.

15. An operations research technique which would be employed to determine the optimum number of window clerks or interviewers to have in an agency serving the public would MOST likely be the use of

   A. line of balance
   B. queueing theory
   C. simulation
   D. work sampling

16. Douglas MacGregor's theory of human motivation classifies worker behavior into two distinct categories: Theory X and Theory Y. Theory X, the traditional view, states that the average man dislikes working and will avoid work if he can, unless coerced. Theory Y holds essentially the opposite view.
    The manager can apply both of these theories to worker behavior BEST if he

   A. follows an *open-door* policy only with respect to his immediate subordinates
   B. recognizes his subordinates' mental and social needs as well as agency needs
   C. recognizes that executive responsibility is primarily limited to fulfillment of agency productivity goals
   D. directs his subordinate managers to follow a policy of close supervision

17. In interpersonal communications, it is important to ascertain whether oral directions and instruction are understood
    One of the MOST important sources of such information is known as

   A. the *halo* effect
   B. evaluation
   C. feedback
   D. quantitative analysis

18. The *grapevine* MOST often provides a useful service by

   A. correcting some of the deficiencies of the formal communication system
   B. rapidly conveying a true picture of events
   C. involving staff in current organizational changes
   D. interfering with the operation of the formal communication system

19. People who are in favor of a leadership style in which the subordinates help make decisions contend that it produces favorable effects in a work unit.
    According to these people, which of the following is NOT likely to be an effect of such *participative management*?

A. Reduced turnover
B. Accelerated learning of duties
C. Greater acceptance of change
D. Reduced acceptance of the work unit's goals

20. Employees of a public service agency will be MOST likely to develop meaningful goals for both the agency and the employee and become committed to attaining them if supervisors

A. allow them unilaterally to set their own goals
B. provide them with a clear understanding of the premises underlying the agency's goals
C. encourage them to concentrate on setting only short-range goals for themselves
D. periodically review the agency's goals in order to suggest changes in accordance with current conditions

20.____

KEY (CORRECT ANSWERS)

1.	B	11.	B
2.	A	12.	D
3.	C	13.	A
4.	D	14.	D
5.	C	15.	B
6.	A	16.	B
7.	B	17.	C
8.	B	18.	A
9.	A	19.	D
10.	D	20.	B

PROGRAM EVALUATION

Table of Contents

	Pages
Program Evaluation Strategy	1
Managing for Success	1
Types of Program Evaluation	1
Judging vs. Coaching	1
Conducting a Program Evaluation	3
The Need for Planning	3
Stage 1 - Evaluability Assessment	3
Performance Measurement	4
Mission, Goals and Objectives	4
Performance Indicators	5
Stage 2 - Designing the Evaluation	6
Stage 3 - Conducting the Study	8
Developing Data Measurement System	8
Determine Data Availability	9
Collecting Data	9
Analyzing Data	10
Data Presentation	10
Refining Measures	10
Stage 4 - Reporting Evaluation Findings	11
Stage 5 - Program Offices Implement Improvement Activities	12
Stage 6 - On-Going Consultation	13

PROGRAM EVALUATION

Program Evaluation Strategy

MANAGING FOR SUCCESS

An essential component of any successful organization is its ability to continually assess and evaluate its performance. To establish effective and efficient programs, managers need fundamental information regarding the position and progress of their programs, and what improvements can be made to enhance the overall quality of their operations.

In identifying this need, the PTO's Office of Planning and Evaluation (P&E) has developed an evaluation strategy for the Patent and Trademark Office. Our goal is to support PTO in planning, assessing, and improving its program activities, so that managers have the information and support they need to continually develop and advance their programs.

TYPES OF PROGRAM EVALUATION

Program evaluation is based on the fundamental idea that programs should have a demonstrable benefit.

In its simplest terms, program evaluation is defined as a systematic approach to assessing the performance of a program or service. Program evaluations are most commonly referred to as either summative or formative in nature. Summative evaluations make a judgment about a program's operations and usefulness, whereas formative evaluations describe a program's operations in order to improve the way in which it functions.

In recent years, the formative approach to evaluating has evolved into what has come to be called "evaluation research."

Evaluation research includes:
- Design of programs
- Ongoing monitoring of how well programs are functioning
- Assessment of program impact
- Analysis of benefits relative to costs.

This approach seems to be the most productive. As internal evaluators, our goal is not only to report to managers on their program's current situation, but also assist them in developing and enhancing the resources they need for continual operational improvement.

JUDGING VS. COACHING

In conducting formative evaluations, the goal is not to judge a program's worth or usefulness, rather the goal is to provide recommendations for program improvements in addition to assessing impacts and results.

A program evaluation trainer, uses the example of a world-class figure-skating champion to differentiate the roles of a coach and judge. As a skater performs, both the judge and the coach are meticulously assessing the skaters every move; however, each has a different motive for evaluating the performance. The judge looks at the performance and impassively scores the skater against the competition, providing little, if any, feedback to the skater. The coach on the other hand, goes a step beyond assessing the performance by actually working with the skater to improve his or her performance. The judge's objective is to score the skater's single performance, whereas the coach's objective is to help the skater achieve his or her fullest potential for future performances.

The coaching perspective helps programs become as efficient and effective as possible, while reaching their fullest potential. Using the example, the coach can work with and recommend improvements to the skater, but it is the skater who is responsible for making the improvements and for eventually becoming a guide and example for others that follow. By diagnosing, consulting and informing programs on their performance, we not only help programs gain a better understanding of what works well within their organization, we also maintain PTO's strategic goal of providing our customers with the highest level of quality and service in all aspects of PTO operations.

Conducting a Program Evaluation

In order to be effective, every evaluation must be tailored to the individual program or organization.

The following are stages in conducting a program evaluation. These stages are designed to adapt to individual needs, interests and the stage of development of the organization or program being evaluated.

THE NEED FOR PLANNING

Ideally, a successful evaluation will provide the best information possible on all key issues within a given set of constraints, such as available time, staff and budget resources. This makes it important to consider at the outset that the design of the evaluation needs to be done carefully, since criticism of the findings will likely focus on the methodology used.

Given the constraints we are all under these days, you may very well ask why you should spend precious resources on planning and designing your evaluation. The answer is precisely because of those constraints. In addition to increasing credibility in the product, a careful and sound design:

- increases overall quality,
- contains costs,
- ensures timeliness of findings,
- increases the strength and specificity of findings and recommendations,
- decreases criticism of methodology,
- improves customer satisfaction, and
- results in less resources required to carry out the evaluation.

STAGE 1: EVALUABILITY ASSESSMENT

Program evaluation is essentially a process in which questions are asked about a program or activity and answers are actively sought. In order to have an effective evaluation--which will result in improved program performance--first, the right questions must be asked, and second, the evaluation team must assure that the questions can be accurately answered.

Before conducting any formal evaluation, an evaluability assessment is conducted. The purpose of the evaluability assessment is to identify the program's goals, performance indicators and data sources, which will be used to conduct the evaluation. The evaluability assessment not only answers the question of whether a program can be meaningfully evaluated, but whether the evaluation is likely to contribute to improved program performance.

During the evaluability assessment there is usually a clear indication of whether a program is ready to be evaluated. If the necessary information (goals, objectives, performance measurements, etc.) is available and is identified by the evaluators and intended users as clear, concise and realistic (given resource allocations and restrictions), the evaluation can proceed. However, if the goals, objectives and performance indicators are found to be either underdeveloped or undefined, the program office is advised to first focus on developing or redefining their performance measurements before continuing with the evaluation.

The foremost question is whether or not the program can be evaluated in a meaningful way based on what currently exists.

Program evaluations are generally concerned with whether a program or policy is achieving its intended goal or purpose. Frequently though, the goals and purposes were to attract as much support as possible for the proposed project, but may lack consistency or be too ambitious given the realities of program functions. Programs and policies that do not have clear and consistent goals can not be evaluated for their effectiveness. Thus, uncovering those goals and purposes is generally the starting point of most evaluations. This first stage of an evaluation is necessary to determine whether they can be evaluated.

Program Evaluation Criteria

- Program goals and objectives, important side effects, and priority information needs are well defined.
- Program goals and objectives are plausible.
- Relevant performance data can be obtained.
- The intended users of the evaluation results have agreed on how they will use the information.

Performance Measurement

Performance measurement is a process by which a program objectively measures how it is accomplishing its mission through the delivery of its products, services, or processes. It is a self-assessment, goal-setting, and progress monitoring tool, which provides on-going performance feedback to both management and staff. A good performance measurement system is designed to provide information which helps clarify goals and motivates performance, solves problems, and corrects deviations or alters planned directions.

Performance Measurement is crucial to the overall management of programs because of one basic principle: "What gets measured, gets done."

Mission, Goals and Objectives

The first step in performance measurement is identifying the mission, goals and objectives. The following is a brief description of each:

The mission is the purpose for which a program or organization was created. A mission answers the following questions:

- Who are we?
- What do we do?
- For whom do we do it?
- Why do we do it?

Goals are statements, usually general and abstract, about how the program expects to accomplish its mission. Goals may be quantitative ("Increase production") or qualitative ("Improve worker morale").

> **Tips on Goal Setting**
> - Goals may be general or specific and may encompass time spans ranging from a few months to several years.
> - Goals may be set for the entire organization, programs, and individuals.
> - Goals at the various organizational levels must be coordinated if the organization is to achieve its intended overall purpose.
> - There must be coordination of the long-term goals of the organization with the short term goals of departments and programs, and of both of these with the personal goals of workers
> - Involve both management and staff when developing goals.

Objectives are the means for accomplishing goals. They must be quantifiable containing specific statements detailing the desired accomplishments of a program's goals.

> **Rules for Writing Objectives**
> - Use a single issue per objective.
> - Define measurable objectives using a verb-noun structure ("Increase productivity by 15 percent by fiscal year 2015").
> - Specify an expected time for achievement.

Performance Indicators

Once goals and objectives have been established, performance indicators are developed. Performance indicators track and measure whether the goals and objectives have been reached, or how well the program is progressing toward achieving them.

In the classical sense, a performance indicator is defined as a ratio where the output of an effort is divided by the inputs (labor, energy, time, etc.) required to produce it. . For example:

$$\frac{\text{\# of customers helped}}{\text{\# of service reps}}$$

$$\frac{\text{\# of acceptable documents produced}}{\text{hours expanded for documents}}$$

> **Customer Requirements and Stakeholder Requirements** are the Building Blocks for Measurement Ratios. When designing indicators ask the question: How Do We Know We Met Customer Requirements?

Two integral components of performance indicators are effectiveness and efficiency. Effective production is defined as producing the desired results, whereas efficient production is defined as producing the desired outputs with a minimum level of input. Simply stated, effectiveness is doing the right things, and efficiency is doing things right.

Effectiveness and efficiency are both critical measures of performance and success. Organizations can temporarily survive without perfect efficiency, but would most likely die if they were ineffective. When designing performance measurements, it is essential that an organization considers both effectiveness and efficiency. Omitting either would result in performance measurements that provide inaccurate and often costly productivity information.

It bears repeating that if a program has not clearly identified its goals and objectives and set effectiveness and efficiency measures, it will be difficult to evaluate.

Four Criteria for Measurement Effectiveness and Efficiency

1. **Quality-** The measure must define and reflect quality of production or services as well as quantity. A measure that assesses only quantity outputs can lead to reduced productivity.

2. **Mission and goals-** The measure must define and assess only outputs and services that are integrated with the organizational mission and strategic goals. Measures directed to products and services that are not consistent with mission and goals threaten productivity.

3. **Rewards and Incentives-** Measures must be integrated with performance incentives, reward systems and practices. Measures that have no important contingencies will not work to improve productivity.

4. **Employee Involvement-** There must be involvement of employees and other direct stakeholders in the definition and construction of productivity measures. When lack of involvement has not resulted in commitment and buy-in, results from the measures are not likely to be received favorably or to have any impact on future productivity.

STAGE 2: DESIGNING THE EVALUATION

What's worth knowing?
How will we get it?
How will it be used?

By the time you have an idea of the evaluation capacity of your program, you may have the answers to many of the questions that lead to the design. Every question asked by an evaluation can be looked at with varying levels of intensity and thoroughness. When great precision is needed and resources are available, the most powerful of evaluations may be conducted, on the other hand when time and resources are limited and only approximate answers are needed, the level of the evaluation will differ. Given the diversity of programs, policies and projects to be evaluated, the number of questions to be answered, and the differing availability of resources, there can be no single recipe for a successful evaluation. However, these simple guidelines, once tailored, should provide a solid framework for conducting an evaluation.

In determining the design of an evaluation, the following questions are answered and an Evaluation Design Proposal is drafted.

1. Why are we doing this evaluation?

Clarify what the overall purpose of the evaluation is and what specific objectives will be accomplished. Focus not only on what the evaluation will do, but also identify what the evaluation will NOT do.

2. For whom are we doing this evaluation?

It is essential to identify who the audience is so that their needs, perspectives and constraints can be assessed. Identify both the primary audience and secondary audiences.

Who is sponsoring the evaluation? Who is authorizing the expenditure of funds and human resources? Who will be approving the report?

3. What are we evaluating?

Discuss the issues of the evaluation. Are we studying the need for a program or activity? The operations of a program or activity? The effects of a program or activity? Define the specific questions to be answered during the evaluation.

4. How are we doing this evaluation?

Make a list of the information needed to conduct the evaluation. Once the information needs are defined, identify the data collection techniques. Examples of Data Collection Techniques:

        Surveys
        Interviews
        Focus Group Sessions
        Case Studies
        Tests
        Observations
        Document Reviews
        Production Reports
        Computerized databases

5. When are we doing this evaluation?

Establish both the beginning and completion dates and interim deadlines. It may be helpful to set up a project plan to track the dates and resources.

6. Where are we doing this evaluation?

Determine the location of the evaluation. Will a special staff be pulled together? Will they need space for meetings? For working? For storage of files?

7. Who is doing this evaluation?

Assess the skills and resources needed to conduct the evaluation. Identify possible training needs and establish roles and responsibilities for each team member (Hendricks, 1994).

Tips on Building an Effective Study Team

- Keep teams small.
- Acknowledge team members' need for high performance.
- Reward both team leaders and team members.
- Focus on people, not methodology.
- Keep a skills inventory of team members.
- Make use of project management tools to create benchmarks of success.
- Form a policy group and a work group to involve policy makers, managers, and key staff in the evaluation.

Consider whether the skills and resources are available internally, or whether it might be more economical or beneficial to hire an external contractor to conduct the evaluation. Depending on the nature of the program or project, it may be critical that the results of the evaluation come from an outside, objective source.

One More Thing

After the design is completed, it is helpful to take an overall look at the design.

A well-designed evaluation can usually be recognized by the way it has:

1. Defined and posed questions for study.
2. Developed the methodological strategies for answering those questions.
3. Formulated a data collection plan that anticipates and addresses problems and obstacles that are likely to be encountered.
4. Provided a detailed analysis plan that will ensure that the questions posed will be answered with the appropriate data in the best possible fashion.
5. Established and maintained focus on the usefulness of the product for the intended user.

A sound design reduces downtime deciding what to do next, reduces time spent on collecting and analyzing irrelevant data and strengthens the relevance of the evaluation.

STAGE 3: CONDUCTING THE STUDY

Once the evaluation proposal is drafted and agreed upon by the evaluation team and the evaluation users, the process of collecting and analyzing the relevant data can begin.

DATA COLLECTION AND ANALYSIS

Developing A Data Measurement System

There are two methods of evaluation studies: qualitative and quantitative. Qualitative data collection systems permit the evaluator to study selected issues, cases, or events in depth and detail; data collection is not constrained by predetermined categories of analysis. Quantitative methods use standardized measures that fit diverse opinions and experiences into predetermined response categories. Considering evaluation design alternatives leads directly to consideration of the relative strengths and weaknesses of qualitative and quantitative studies, and the time and resources available for the study.

The advantage of the quantitative approach is that it measures the reactions of a great many people to a limited set of questions, thus facilitating comparison and statistical aggregation of the data. It gives a broad, generalized set of findings. Qualitative methods typically produce a wealth of detailed data about a much smaller number of people and cases. Qualitative data provide depth and detail through direct quotation and careful description of program situations, events, people, interactions, and observed behaviors.

Purposes and functions of qualitative and quantitative data are different, yet can be complementary. The statistics from standardized items make summaries, comparisons, and generalizations quite easy and precise. The narrative comments from open-ended questions are typically meant to provide a forum for elaboration, explanations, meanings, and new ideas.

It is recommended that an evaluation team engage stakeholders early because they have a different perspective, have data the evaluator needs, and can influence the evaluation positively if they are engaged, or negatively if they are ignored or threatened.

Categorizing research questions into major categories can help refine the research agenda of almost any study. Time spent in developing a detailed research design, data collection and analysis plan may improve the quality of the overall results.

Stakeholders include potential users of evaluation information and those with an investment in the organization or unit involved in the study.

Determine Data Availability

Once it has been established what to measure, it must be determined if the data for those measures is available and how to get it. If data is not available, alternative indicators must be identified.

The evaluation team should try to keep its indicators simple and use existing data whenever possible. However, do not compromise the evaluation by discarding indicators the team thinks are meaningful and important before weighing their obtainability.

Data Availability Concerns

1. Does the data currently exist ? If not, can it be developed, and at what effort and cost?
2. If the data exists, what will it cost to retrieve the data?
3. What will it take to get the data converted into the established measurement values?
4. Will a system investment be required? At what cost?
5. Will management support this level of cost? Can a limited version be used?
6. When will data be produced?

Collecting Data

The collection of data addresses the critical issues of making sure the correct data is identified, and a baseline is collected. The baseline data reflects the initial status of the program or process. During this phase, in addition to documenting the method of collection of the data, document any problems with the process, and work to resolve any process problems regularly. Meet with management at the end of an established trial period to evaluate results.

Analyzing Data

Once we have collected the data and before we meet with management, we must analyze the data to make sure that it will provide us with enough information and the right type of information on which to base an evaluation. We must ensure that the data fits the indicators identified to analyze. Agree to finalize the current indicators or revise them as needed, and analyze the baseline data collected for the purpose of setting goals.

DATA PRESENTATION

Once the data has been collected and analyzed, it must be decided how the data and results will be presented. Numbers by themselves are often difficult to understand, they cannot explain circumstances, and they may not easily lead to conclusions. Therefore, it is important to present the information in ways that make it easy to understand, that show relationships to other data, and that allow the information to be used to support decision-making processes. Whenever possible, use graphical tools to present data.

Measures must be shown in context. The most frequent evaluation contexts are: (1) goals compared to actual results, (2) trends in relation to previous periodic results, and (3) comparison of results to other relevant data. Using one or more of these contexts, meaningful conclusions should be drawn about the measurement result with little or no explanation.

REFINING MEASURES

Indicators may need some slight modifications or adjustment to better meet performance information needs of program or executive management. Continually check the usefulness of measurement data and adjust data collection methods if necessary.

Adjusting Measures

Are the measures working well?
What are the measures indicating?
Are additional indicators necessary?
Is data not really available (too difficult or expensive to acquire)?
Is data too difficult to use?

Balance Types Of Measures

One consideration of performance indicator development is that measures are interrelated and cannot be viewed in isolation. Timeliness, quality and cost are always in contention with each other, and the impact of improving any one or two must be weighed in relation to the expense of the third. A balance must be reached between the effectiveness and the economy and efficiency.

Consider Weighting Measures

Not all indicators are equally important. To reflect importance or priorities within measures or categories of measures, weight or index the measures. Weighting or indexing measures is an involved and advanced process and may not be necessary or appropriate for every program. However, weighting measures can provide some valuable insights into program outcomes.

Integrating with Management Process

Once performance results become available, the challenge shifts to presenting and using them effectively.

Establish Goals

Goals should be established based on: (1) policy or administrative priorities, (2) mission (3) customer feedback, (4) past history, (5) forecasted demand and (6) benchmark information.

Determine What The Measurements Say

It is extremely important to understand what the measurements say, as well as what they do not say. The measurements must be compared to performance goals, benchmarks, or past performance. Then variances or changes must be analyzed, and subsequent actions must be planned. In addition to program performance evaluation, the measurement results in the evaluation process can be used for external reporting, planning and budgeting activities and performance appraisal evaluation.

STAGE 4: REPORTING EVALUATION RESULTS

Reporting evaluation results is more of a process than a stage. Beginning on the first day of the evaluation, the evaluators should be continually reporting and discussing their findings with the evaluation users. It is not only important to keep them updated on the evaluation's progress, but also, it is important to keep them informed of any findings and recommendations that can be implemented before the full completion of the evaluation. Remember, the reason for doing an evaluation is to help an organization or program become as effective and efficient as possible. The sooner an organization can implement changes or improvements, the better.

Action-Oriented Reporting

As stated previously, the purpose of an evaluation is to improve a program or an organization's performance. The way in which evaluators do this is by providing recommendations for improvement to management and staff.

The majority of an evaluation report should be devoted to communicating the findings and specific recommendations. Reports should be action-oriented, centered mostly around the findings, but also around the recommendations and suggestions for implementation.

Action-oriented reports are often structured as a series of short reports targeted to specific audiences, rather than one all inclusive document.

Findings and recommendations should be presented clearly and concisely, in a way that meets the informational needs of the audience. In order for recommendations to be accepted by an organization, it must first understand what is being recommended and why it is relevant to their concerns. Evaluation studies are only useful if they are used.

Program Evaluation Report

Generally, an evaluation report should include:
- Executive Summary
  Purpose of Evaluation
  Program Background
  Evaluation Methodology
- Analysis of the Findings
- Recommendations

Tips for Reporting Evaluation Results

- Remember that the burden for effectively reporting results is on the evaluators, not the audience.
- Be aggressive. Instead of waiting for audiences to request information, actively look for opportunities to report results. Report regularly and frequently, appear in person if at all possible, and target multiple reports and briefings to specific audiences and /or issues.
- Simplify, simplify! Audiences are usually busy and their interest is pulled in different directions, so determine and report on the key points. If the core message creates interest, quickly follow up with more details.
- Study the audience. Learn about their backgrounds, interests, concerns, plans, pet peeves, etc.
- Focus on actions. Audiences are rarely interested in general information; they usually want guidance that will help them decide what to do next.
- Report in many different ways. Rather than using only one reporting technique or another, produce several different types of reports. Use written reports, personal briefings, screen show presentations, etc.

STAGE 5: PROGRAM OFFICES IMPLEMENT IMPROVEMENT ACTIVITIES

In this phase of the evaluation process, program office managers implement and monitor the recommendations and action plans originating from the evaluation study. The program manager facilitates the solution of problems by motivating staff and providing technical support. Particular attention must be given to customer and stakeholder requirements.

All employees should be trained in the process improvement recommendations so that they will possess the skills needed to recommend solutions to future problems. Decisions made closer to the customer and occurrence of events save time, reduce errors, and improve morale and service.

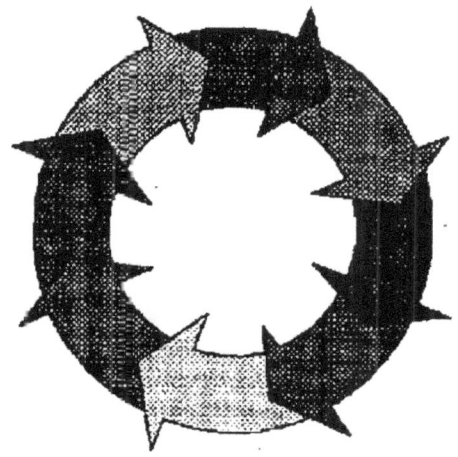

STAGE 6: ON-GOING CONSULTATION

Program evaluation is a continuous process of measuring, analyzing and refining an organization or program's performance.

A program evaluation is not an end in itself, rather it is the beginning of a continuous self-evaluation mechanism. With an effective evaluation comes additional data, refined measurements and new initiatives. In order to remain effective, organizations must continually evaluate this information to ensure the achievement of their mission, goals, and objectives.

GLOSSARY OF PROJECT MANAGEMENT

A

Agile software development is a set of fundamental principles about how software should be developed based on an agile way of working in contrast to previous heavy-handed software development methodologies.

Aggregate planning is an operational activity which does an aggregate plan for the production process, in advance of 2 to 18 months, to give an idea to management as to what quantity of materials and other resources are to be procured and when, so that the total cost of operations of the organization is kept to the minimum over that period.

Allocation is the assignment of available resources in an economic way.

B

Budget generally refers to a list of all planned expenses and revenues.

Budgeted cost of work performed (BCWP) measures the budgeted cost of work that has actually been performed, rather than the cost of work scheduled.

Budgeted cost of work scheduled (BCWS) the approved budget that has been allocated to complete a scheduled task (or Work Breakdown Structure (WBS) component) during a specific time period.

Business model is a profit-producing system that has an important degree of independence from the other systems within an enterprise.

Business analysis is the set of tasks, knowledge, and techniques required to identify business needs and determine solutions to business problems. Solutions often include a systems development component, but may also consist of process improvement or organizational change.

Business operations are those ongoing recurring activities involved in the running of a business for the purpose of producing value for the stakeholders. They are contrasted with project management, and consist of business processes.

Business process is a collection of related, structured activities or tasks that produce a specific service or product (serve a particular goal) for a particular customer or customers. There are three types of business processes: Management processes, Operational processes, and Supporting processes.

Business Process Modeling (BPM) is the activity of representing processes of an enterprise, so that the current ("as is") process may be analyzed and improved in future ("to be").

C

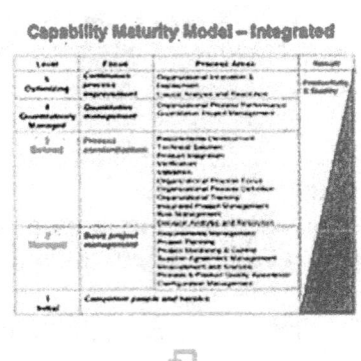

Capability Maturity Model.

Capability Maturity Model (CMM) in software engineering is a model of the maturity of the capability of certain business processes. A maturity model can be described as a structured collection of elements that describe certain aspects of maturity in an organization, and aids in the definition and understanding of an organization's processes.

Change control is the procedures used to ensure that changes (normally, but not necessarily, to IT systems) are introduced in a controlled and coordinated manner. Change control is a major aspect of the broader discipline of change management.

Change management is a field of management focused on organizational changes. It aims to ensure that methods and procedures are used for efficient and prompt handling of all changes to controlled IT infrastructure, in order to minimize the number and impact of any related incidents upon service.

Case study is a research method which involves an in-depth, longitudinal examination of a single instance or event: a case. They provide a systematic way of looking at events, collecting data, analyzing information, and reporting the results.

Certified Associate in Project Management is an entry-level certification for project practitioners offered by Project Management Institute.

Communications Log is an on-going documentation of communication events between any identified project stakeholders, managed and collected by the project manager that describes: the sender and receiver of the communication event; where, when and for how long the communication event elapsed; in what form the communication event took place; a summary of what information was communicated; what actions/outcomes should be taken as a result of the communication event; and to what level of priority should the actions/outcomes of the communication event be graded

Constructability is a project management technique to review the construction processes from start to finish during pre-construction phrase. It will identify obstacles before a project is actually built to reduce or prevent error, delays, and cost overrun.

Costs in economics, business, and accounting are the value of money that has been used up to produce something, and hence is not available for use anymore. In business, the cost may be one of acquisition, in which case the amount of money expended to acquire it is counted as cost.

Cost engineering is the area of engineering practice where engineering judgment and experience are used in the application of scientific principles and techniques to problems of cost estimating, cost control, business planning and management science, profitability analysis, project management, and planning and scheduling."[1]

Construction, in the fields of architecture and civil engineering, is a process that consists of the building or assembling of infrastructure. Far from being a single activity, large scale construction is a feat of multitasking. Normally the job is managed by the project manager and supervised by the construction manager, design engineer, construction engineer or project architect.

Cost overrun is defined as excess of actual cost over budget.

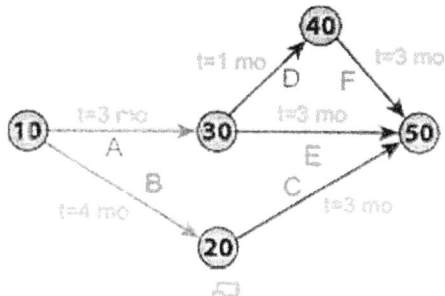

PERT chart with two critical paths.

Critical path method (CPM) is a mathematically based modeling technique for scheduling a set of project activities, used in project management.

Critical chain project management (CCPM) is a method of planning and managing projects that puts more emphasis on the resources required to execute project tasks.

D

Dependency in a project network is a link amongst a project's terminal elements.

Dynamic Systems Development Method (DSDM) is a software development methodology originally based upon the Rapid Application Development methodology. DSDM is an iterative and incremental approach that emphasizes continuous user involvement.

Duration of a project's terminal element is the number of calendar periods it takes from the time the execution of element starts to the moment it is completed.

Deliverable A contractually required work product, produced and delivered to a required state. A deliverable may be a document, hardware, software or other tangible product.

E

Earned schedule (ES) is an extension to earned value management (EVM), which renames two traditional measures, to indicate clearly they are in units of currency or quantity, not time.

Earned value management (EVM) is a project management technique for measuring project progress in an objective manner, with a combination of measuring scope, schedule, and cost in a single integrated system.

Effort management is a project management subdiscipline for effective and efficient use of time and resources to perform activities regarding quantity, quality and direction.

Enterprise modeling is the process of understanding an enterprise business and improving its performance through creation of enterprise models. This includes the modelling of the relevant business domain (usually relatively stable), business processes (usually more volatile), and Information technology

Estimation in project management is the processes of making accurate estimates using the appropriate techniques.

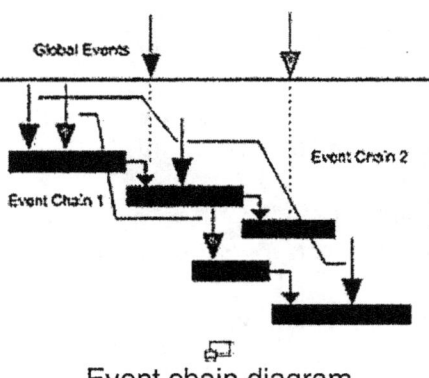
Event chain diagram

Event chain diagram : diagram that show the relationships between events and tasks and how the events affect each other.

Event chain methodology is an uncertainty modeling and schedule network analysis technique that is focused on identifying and managing events and event chains that affect project schedules.

Extreme project management (XPM) refers to a method of managing very complex and very uncertain projects.

F

Float in a project network is the amount of time that a task in a project network can be delayed without causing a delay to subsequent tasks and or the project completion date.

Focused improvement in Theory of Constraints is the ensemble of activities aimed at elevating the performance of any system, especially a business system, with respect to its goal by eliminating its constraints one by one and by not working on non-constraints.

Fordism, named after Henry Ford, refers to various social theories. It has varying but related meanings in different fields, and for Marxist and non-Marxist scholars.

G

Henry Gantt was an American mechanical engineer and management consultant, who developed the Gantt chart in the 1910s.

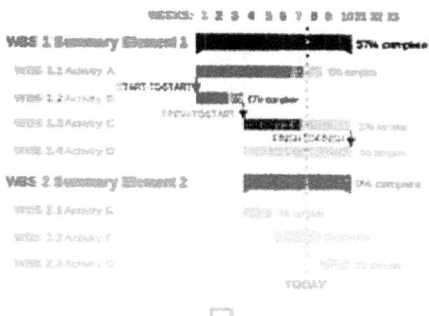

A Gantt chart.

Gantt chart is a type of bar chart that illustrates a project schedule. It illustrate the start and finish dates of the terminal elements and summary elements of a project. Terminal elements and summary elements comprise the work breakdown structure of the project.

Goal or objective consists of a projected state of affairs which a person or a system plans or intends to achieve or bring about — a personal or organizational desired end-point in some sort of assumed development. Many people endeavor to reach goals within a finite time by setting deadlines

Goal setting involves establishing specific, measurable and time targeted objectives

Graphical Evaluation and Review Technique (GERT) is a network analysis technique that allows probabilistic treatment of both network logic and activity duration estimated.

H

Hammock activity is a grouping of subtasks that "hangs" between two end dates it is tied to (or the two end-events it is fixed to).

HERMES is a Project Management Method developed by the Swiss Government, based on the German V-Modell. The first domain of application was software projects.

I

Integrated Master Plan (IMP) is an event-based, top level plan, consisting of a hierarchy of Program Events.

ISO 10006 is a guidelines for quality management in projects, is an international standard developed by the International Organization for Standardization.

Iterative and Incremental development is a cyclic software development process developed in response to the weaknesses of the waterfall model. It starts with an initial planning and ends with deployment with the cyclic interaction in between

K

Kickoff meeting is the first meeting with the project team and the client of the project.

L

Level of Effort (LOE) is qualified as a support type activity which doesn't lend itself to measurement of a discrete accomplishment. Examples of such an activity may be project budget accounting, customer liaison, etc.

Linear scheduling method (LSM) is a graphical scheduling method focusing on continuous resource utilization in repetitive activities. It is believed that it originally adopted the idea of Line-Of-Balance method.

Lean manufacturing or lean production, which is often known simply as "Lean", is the practice of a theory of production that considers the expenditure of resources for any means other than the creation of value for the presumed customer to be wasteful, and thus a target for elimination.

M

Management in business and human organization activity is simply the act of getting people together to accomplish desired goals. Management comprises planning, organizing, staffing, leading or directing, and controlling an organization (a group of one or more people or entities) or effort for the purpose of accomplishing a goal.

Management process is a process of planning and controlling the performance or execution of any type of activity.

Management science (MS), is the discipline of using mathematical modeling and other analytical methods, to help make better business management decisions.

Megaproject is an extremely large-scale investment project.

Motivation is the set of reasons that prompts one to engage in a particular behavior.

N

Nonlinear Management (NLM) is a superset of management techniques and strategies that allows order to emerge by giving organizations the space to self-organize, evolve and adapt, encompassing Agile, Evolutionary and Lean approaches, as well as many others.

O

Operations management is an area of business that is concerned with the production of good quality goods and services, and involves the responsibility of ensuring that business operations are efficient and effective. It is the management of resources, the distribution of goods and services to customers, and the analysis of queue systems.

Operations, see **Business operations**

Operations Research (OR) is an interdisciplinary branch of applied mathematics and formal science that uses methods such as mathematical modeling, statistics, and algorithms to arrive at optimal or near optimal solutions to complex problems.

Organization is a social arrangement which pursues collective goals, which controls its own performance, and which has a boundary separating it from its environment.

Organization development (OD) is a planned, structured, organization-wide effort to increase the organization's effectiveness and health.

P

Planning in organizations and public policy is both the organizational process of creating and maintaining a plan; and the psychological process of thinking about the activities required to create a desired goal on some scale.

Portfolio in finance is an appropriate mix of or collection of investments held by an institution or a private individual.

PRINCE2 : PRINCE2 is a project management methodology. The planning, monitoring and control of all aspects of the project and the motivation of all those involved in it to achieve the project objectives on time and to the specified cost, quality and performance.

Process is an ongoing collection of activities, with an inputs, outputs and the energy required to transform inputs to outputs.

Process architecture is the structural design of general process systems and applies to fields such as computers (software, hardware, networks, etc.), business processes (enterprise architecture, policy and procedures, logistics, project management, etc.), and any other process system of varying degrees of complexity.

Process management is the ensemble of activities of planning and monitoring the performance of a process, especially in the sense of business process, often confused with reengineering.

Product breakdown structure (PBS) in project management is an exhaustive, hierarchical tree structure of components that make up an item, arranged in whole-part relationship.

Product description in project management is a structured format of presenting information about a project product

Program Evaluation and Review Technique (PERT) is a statistical tool, used in project management, designed to analyze and represent the tasks involved in completing a given project.

Program Management is the process of managing multiple ongoing inter-dependent projects. An example would be that of designing, manufacturing and providing support infrastructure for an automobile manufacturer.

Project : A temporary endeavor undertaken to create a unique product, service, or result.

Project accounting Is the practice of creating financial reports specifically designed to track the financial progress of projects, which can then be used by managers to aid project management.

Project Cost Management A method of managing a project in real-time from the estimating stage to project control; through the use of technology cost, schedule and productivity is monitored.

Project management : The complete set of tasks, techniques, tools applied during project execution'.

Project Management Body of Knowledge (PMBOK) : The sum of knowledge within the profession of project management that is standardized by ISO.

Project management office: The Project management office in a business or professional enterprise is the department or group that defines and maintains the standards of process, generally related to project management, within the organization. The PMO strives to standardize and introduce economies of repetition in the execution of projects. The PMO is the source of documentation, guidance and metrics on the practice of project management and execution.

Project management process is the management process of planning and controlling the performance or execution of a project.

Project Management Professional is a certificated professional in project management.

Project Management Simulators are computer-based tools used in project management training programs. Usually, project management simulation is a group exercise. The computer-based simulation is an interactive learning activity.

Project management software is a type of software, including scheduling, cost control and budget management, resource allocation, collaboration software, communication, quality management and documentation or administration systems, which are used to deal with the complexity of large projects.

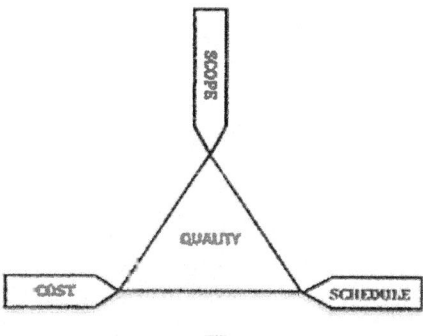

Project Management Triangle

Project Management Triangle is a model of the constraints of project management.

Project manager : professional in the field of project management. Project managers can have the responsibility of the planning, execution, and closing of any project, typically relating to construction industry, architecture, computer networking, telecommunications or software development.

Project network is a graph (flow chart) depicting the sequence in which a project's terminal elements are to be completed by showing terminal elements and their dependencies.

Project plan is a formal, approved document used to guide both *project execution* and *project control*. The primary uses of the project plan are to document planning assumptions and decisions, facilitate communication among *stakeholders*, and document approved scope, cost, and schedule *baselines*. A project plan may be summary or detailed.

Project planning is part of project management, which relates to the use of schedules such as Gantt charts to plan and subsequently report progress within the project environment.

Project stakeholders are those entities within or without an organization which sponsor a project or, have an interest or a gain upon a successful completion of a project.

Project team is the management team leading the project, and provide services to the project. Projects often bring together a variety number of problems. Stakeholders have important issues with others.

Proport refers to the combination of the unique skills of an organisation's members for collective advantage.

Q

Quality can mean a high degree of excellence ("a quality product"), a degree of excellence or the lack of it ("work of average quality"), or a property of something ("the addictive quality of alcohol").[1] Distinct from the vernacular, the subject of this article is the business interpretation of quality.

Quality, Cost, Delivery(QCD) as used in lean manufacturing measures a businesses activity and develops Key performance indicators. QCD analysis often forms a part of continuous improvement programs

R

Reengineering is radical redesign of an organization's processes, especially its business processes. Rather than organizing a firm into functional specialties (like production, accounting, marketing, etc.) and considering the tasks that each function performs; complete processes from materials acquisition, to production, to marketing and distribution should be considered. The firm should be re-engineered into a series of processes.

Resources are what is required to carry out a project's tasks. They can be people, equipment, facilities, funding, or anything else capable of definition (usually other than labour) required for the completion of a project activity.

Risk is the precise probability of specific eventualities.

Risk management is a management specialism aiming to reduce different risks related to a preselected domain to the level accepted by society. It may refer to numerous types of threats caused by environment, technology, humans, organizations and politics.

Risk register is a tool commonly used in project planning and organizational risk assessments.

S

Schedules in project management consists of a list of a project's terminal elements with intended start and finish dates.

Scientific management is a theory of management that analyzes and synthesizes workflow processes, improving labor productivity.

Scope of a project in project management is the sum total of all of its products and their requirements or features.

Scope creep refers to uncontrolled changes in a project's scope. This phenomenon can occur when the scope of a project is not properly defined, documented, or controlled. It is generally considered a negative occurrence that is to be avoided.

The systems development life cycle.

Scrum is an iterative incremental process of software development commonly used with agile software development. Despite the fact that "Scrum" is not an acronym, some companies implementing the process have been known to adhere to an all capital letter expression of the word, i.e. SCRUM.

Six Sigma is a business management strategy, originally developed by Motorola, that today enjoys widespread application in many sectors of industry.

Software engineering is the application of a systematic, disciplined, quantifiable approach to the development, operation and maintenance of software.[1]

Systems Development Life Cycle (SDLC) is any logical process used by a systems analyst to develop an information system, including requirements, validation, training, and user ownership. An SDLC should result in a high quality system that meets or exceeds customer expectations, within time and cost estimates, works effectively and efficiently in the current and planned Information Technology infrastructure, and is cheap to maintain and cost-effective to enhance.

Systems engineering is an interdisciplinary field of engineering that focuses on how complex engineering projects should be designed and managed.

T

Task is part of a set of actions which accomplish a job, problem or assignment.

Tasks in project management are activity that needs to be accomplished within a defined period of time.

Task analysis is the analysis or a breakdown of exactly how a task is accomplished, such as what sub-tasks are required

Timeline is a graphical representation of a chronological sequence of events, also referred to as a chronology. It can also mean a schedule of activities, such as a timetable.

U

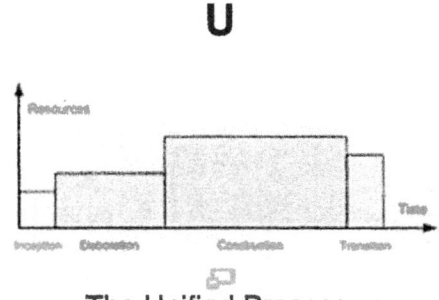

The Unified Process.

Unified Process: The Unified process is a popular iterative and incremental software development process framework. The best-known and extensively documented refinement of the Unified Process is the Rational Unified Process (RUP).

V

Value engineering (VE) is a systematic method to improve the "value" of goods and services by using an examination of function. Value, as defined, is the ratio of function to cost. Value can therefore be increased by either improving the function or reducing the cost. It is a primary tenet of value engineering that basic functions be preserved and not be reduced as a consequence of pursuing value improvements.

Vertical slice is a type of milestone, benchmark, or deadline, with emphasis on demonstrating progress across all components of a project.

Virtual Design and Construction (VDC) is the use of integrated multi-disciplinary performance models of design-construction projects, including the Product (i.e., facilities), Work Processes and Organization of the design - construction - operation team in order to support explicit and public business objectives.

W

Wideband Delphi is a consensus-based estimation technique for estimating effort.

Work in project management is the amount of effort applied to produce a deliverable or to accomplish a task (a terminal element).

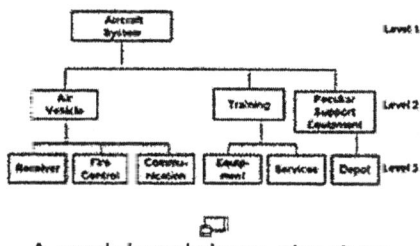

A work breakdown structure.

Work Breakdown Structure (WBS) is a tool that defines a project and groups the project's discrete work elements in a way that helps organize and define the total work scope of the project. A Work breakdown structure element may be a product, data, a service, or any combination. WBS also provides the necessary framework for detailed cost estimating and control along with providing guidance for schedule development and control.

Work package is a subset of a project that can be assigned to a specific party for execution. Because of the similarity, work packages are often misidentified as projects.

Workstream is a set of associated activities, focused around a particular scope that follow a path from initiation to completion.

CPSIA information can be obtained
at www.ICGtesting.com
Printed in the USA
LVHW060024300121
677862LV00009B/916